Monographic Sociology of Dimitrie Gusti

Europäische Hochschulschriften

European University Studies

Publications Universitaires Européennes

Reihe XXII   **Soziologie**
Series XXII   Sociology
Série XXII   Sociologie

Volume/Band **454**

Gabriela Felicia Georgevici

Monographic Sociology of Dimitrie Gusti

Social Science and Reform

Bibliographic Information published by the Deutsche Nationalbibliothek
The Deutsche Nationalbibliothek lists this publication in the Deutsche
Nationalbibliografie; detailed bibliographic data is available in the internet at
http://dnb.d-nb.de.

Translated by Monica Rosu

ISSN 0721-3379
ISBN 978-3-631-64566-6 (Print)
E-ISBN 978-3-653-03758-6 (E-Book)
DOI 10.3726/978-3-653-03758-6

© Peter Lang GmbH
Internationaler Verlag der Wissenschaften
Frankfurt am Main 2013
All rights reserved.
Peter Lang Edition is an Imprint of Peter Lang GmbH.

Peter Lang – Frankfurt am Main · Bern · Bruxelles · New York ·
Oxford · Warszawa · Wien

All parts of this publication are protected by copyright. Any
utilisation outside the strict limits of the copyright law, without
the permission of the publisher, is forbidden and liable to
prosecution. This applies in particular to reproductions,
translations, microfilming, and storage and processing in
electronic retrieval systems.

This book was peer reviewed prior to publication.

www.peterlang.com

Table of Contents

Abbreviations List 7

Preface 9

Chapter I
Social science and reform. Idea championed by
the Bucharest Sociology School 11
1. Doctrine and method of the Bucharest Sociology School 14
2. Monographic sociology– science of social reality 19
3. Sociologic monograph 23

Chapter II
Development stages of the Romanian Sociology School 37
1. The stage of the Bucharest Sociologic School 38
2. Superior School of Social Work 56

Chapter III
The Banat-Crişana Social Institute –
promoter and innovator of the research ideas and
methods initiated by the Bucharest Sociologic School 61
1. Constitution and organisation of the Banat –
   Crişana Social Institute 61

Chapter IV
The Banat-Crişana Social Institute monographic campaigns 77
1. The Belinţ campaign 77
2. The Sârbova campaign 88
3. The Pojejena de Jos campaign 93
4. The Ohaba Bistra campaign 94
5. The Almăj Valley campaign 98

6. The Naidăș campaign 105

Conclusions 109

Bibliography 111

Annex 123

Abbreviations List

MIBC	– Monographic investigation in the Belinț commune
T.C.L.	– Timiș County Library
B.C.S.I	– Banat-Crișana Social Institute
R.S.I. .	– Romanian Social Institute
M.B.M.A.	– Mountain Banat Museum Archive
SCM	– Sârbova commune monograph
J.B.C.S.I	– Journal of the Banat-Crișana Social Institute

Preface

The work "*Monographic Sociology of Dimitrie Gusti. Social Science and Reform"* aims at bringing back to the specialists' attention an important moment of the history of Romanian sociology, which is still highly relevant, both as regards the idea promoted by the Bucharest Sociologic School and the Banat-Crișana Social Institute, and as regards the virtues of the method of sociologic monograph.

The first part is dedicated to the synthetic presentation of the *Bucharest Sociologic School*, focused on the *science and reform* programme. The analysis of the significance of the "Bucharest Sociologic School" paradigm constitutes the fundamental construction of the work, starting from what Professor Dimitrie Gusti understood by sociologic monograph – synthesis in time and space of a corner of the earth, which, beyond the philosophic perspective, challenges us to attempt a tri-dimensional comprehension in time, as global view meant to correlate traditions of the past with the present reality, but also with the opportunities of the future.

On the basis of an ample documentation from the most diverse sources, the book forwards a detailed presentation of the monographs conducted by the Bucharest School, with their specific characteristics, of Professor Dimitrie Gusti and the other remarkable personalities of the Romanian scientific elite in the inter-war period, animated by the desire to know and act for the modernisation of the social realities and the life of Romanians. The work presents the stages completed in the vast process of building the "social science and reform", starting with the Yassy seminar of sociology, continuing with the publicist activity, public conferences, monographic campaigns conducted by the interdisciplinary teams, the creation of institutions, among which the Romanian Social Institute, the School of Social Work and Assistance, and the Law of the Social Service.

The second part brings an important contribution to the comprehension of the Romanian sociology movement, i.e. the *Banat-Crișana Social Institute,* but also to the process of coagulation of the Banat sociology, after a long period of rupture generated by history. Beside the already accumulated literature, the work is based on a meticulous analysis of the archives and reports of previous researches, of the relevant statistic data, brining important contributions to the understanding of a highly important regional sociologic initiative. The Banat-Crişana Social Institute, enhanced by the adoption of the Gustian programme, was crystallised and developed under difficult circumstances related to human and economic factors, representing in fact a true heroic act, built around a noble idea. Furthermore, the chapter presents a rigorously documented analysis of the genesis and evolution of a sociologic institution, of the intellectual, cultural and political context, of the organisational structure, and also of its programme. The work is a review of the research campaigns of the Banat group, impressive in their scope if we consider the scarcity of resources. The analysis reveals the driving force of this initiative of historic importance for the Romanian sociology: striving with enthusiasm and assuming social responsibilities way beyond the scarcity of resources.

The author

Chapter I
Social science and reform. Idea championed by the Bucharest Sociology School

Dimitrie Gusti is known as the founder of sociology doctrine and school, the initiator and organiser of the action of sociological research of Romanian social reality, founder of the "Association for social science and reform" that later became "The Romanian Social Institute", creator of the Bucharest Village Museum, Chairman the Romanian Academy, member of the French Institute, founder and leader of journals. He was a scientific personality of great erudition in the social and philosophical fields.

Dimitrie Gusti was trained as sociologist in Germany's intellectual climate and distinguished himself in the Romanian sociology not only as a cabinet researcher, but as a scientist preoccupied by the organised study of the inter-war Romanian village.

Dimitrie Gusti's professional vocation is rooted in his academic training, the German cultural milieu having influenced his way of thinking and acting. "In 1899 he left for Berlin (Germany) determined to study philosophy, especially – as himself put it in his "autobiography" at the end of his PhD thesis – *social philosophy*. We should mention in this respect that for his sociologic formation D. Gusti set out to study, for the elaboration of his PhD thesis, all "humanities". In order to study the history of philosophy, Gusti chose as professor and co-ordinator of his PhD thesis the famous Friederic Paulsen (1846 – 1908), author of an introductory manual to the study of philosophy, renowned in the whole word, conceived as a "Philosophia militans" (after the medieval model of an "ecclesia militans"), formula that Gusti will retain and use as title for his work "Sociologia Militans". As professors and guides of his PhD he did not choose only philosophy professors, but also other specialists in social sciences, i.e. the psychologist Wilhelm Wundt (1832 – 1920), whose studies suggested him the introduction in his sociological system of the idea of "law of sociological parallelism", as well as the economist

Karl Bucher (1847 – 1900) and the historian Karl Lamprech (1856 – 1915), from whom he took and introduced in his system the concepts of "cosmological frame" and "historical frame". Furthermore, he also studied law, choosing for that matter the Criminology Seminar taught by professor Franz von Liset (1851 – 1919), and thoroughly studied legal sciences, which suggested him the idea of the existence of "legal manifestations" with the role of "social life" regulators of (Chipea, F., 2008, pp. 23 – 24).

In his work "Essay on Goethe" professor D. Gusti claimed: "Goethe's work and life have always had an extraordinary ascendant upon me and I owe them mostly of my soul and personality formation. (…) It is Goethe who taught me the dynamic lesson I have never forgotten of life courage, civilisation, boldness and modesty" (Gusti, D., 1971, p. 57).

Dimitrie Gusti's fundamental thinking was crystallised under the influence of Wundt's teachings, as he was attracted by concrete ethical preoccupations (Vulcănescu, M., 1998, p. 34):

1) The "realistic critical neo-Kantian" philosophical standpoint;
2) "The idea of the opposition between natural and spiritual worlds, between nature and culture" – and the need to explain this opposition. As D. Gusti's point of view was different from Wundt's, "the key of the relations between the two worlds" is society;
3) the will is the "substrate of social manifestations";
4) the fundamental idea of Gustian ethics is *"the ascension of man through his own deeds", "Werde was du bist"*.

Dimitrie Gusti was a professor in Yassy until 1920, when he transferred to the chair of sociology, ethics and politics at the Faculty of Letters in Bucharest, where he distinguished himself by the fact he succeeded in creating a scientific movement of large proportions, and created a true "school", The Bucharest Sociology School.

Between the two World Wars, the "Monographic school" created and guided by professor D. Gusti set the corner stones of Romanian modern sociology, with an important international echo in the sociology field of the time. It is characterised by the systematic organisation of campaigns for direct research of social reality with "complex inter-disciplinary teams", initially organised within the Seminar of Sociology of the

Sociology Chair within the University of Bucharest, and then expanded throughout the country grace to a network of institutes.

The principles underlying the research, still valid nowadays, through the rules of a good research, i.e.: theoretic training, sincerity and objectivity to the facts, exact, complete, controlled and verified observation, researchers' documentation, multidisciplinary teams, comparison of phenomena, all are testimonies of Professor Gusti's originality.

Major personality of his epoch, world-wide famous scientist, man of culture, D. Gusti imposed himself nationally and globally as a sociologist, and the "prestigious place he occupied is due not so much to his doctrine, interesting and full of ideas as it may be, but rather to the initiation, organisation and co-ordination – together with a team of active collaborators – of the research of social realities in our country" (Gusti, D., 1965, p. 57).

Assessing the influence of Dimitrie Gusti's scientific personality in Romanian sociology and society, Professor Cătălin Zamfir, in his work "What is Dimitrie Gusti's legacy to post-war sociology?" (Zamfir, C., 2005, pp. 11 – 14) presents four great directions he identified:

- "D. Gusti created sociology as a science in Romania, with international prestige and a wide national coverage and involvement.
- Second, D. Gusti conceived sociology as a science of the nation, with the mission of contributing to the self-awareness of Romanian society and thus to the project of social modernisation. Hence a predominantly descriptive and empirical orientation, nevertheless based on a top theoretic frame. (…)
- Third, D Gusti engaged Romanian society in social reform, which continued to have a great influence after 1945 too.
- The fourth direction of influence refers to the creation of a strong sociology school, which survived the instauration of communism, being constructed according to the pre-war model".

The work of Professor Dimitrie Gusti highlights its value through practical action as well, i.e. the deployment of actions meant to achieve the sociologic monographying of social reality involving university teachers, students and specialists in the most various fields.

1. Doctrine and method of the Bucharest Sociology School

Creator of a sociologic system, Dimitrie Gusti is original in the way he conceived social reality and sociology as a science. Like other sociologists, he had grasped the fact that sociology could no longer ignore reality.

Sociology is the science of social reality. Social reality, according to Professor D. Gusti, "is the basis on which an epoch's objective culture and institutions are erected (...) constitutes a complex of parallel manifestations of autonomous social units, conditioned by natural and social frames and justified by social will. It has permanent links with the environment, which imprints its continual modifications and upon which it acts by its own will power" (Gusti, D., 1968, p. 236). He claims that social reality is a combination of various innumerable social units: family, village, town , churches, schools etc., that are "combined in different variants in more and more comprising units of nations, states, empires" (Gusti, D., 1940, p. 3).

Professor Dimitrie Gusti (Gusti, D., 1968, pp. 238 – 239) affirmed that sociology is the sciences of "society as an entirety", whereas social reality is "a complex system of parallel frames and manifestations of social units". The social is considered a conjecture of spatial, temporal, vital and spiritual circumstances that constitute the *frames or the environment,* more precisely cosmological, historic, biologic and psychological. By frames he understands the four elements forming the two categories: *"the natural category"* and *"the social category"*. The natural category, made of the *"cosmic frame"* and the *"biologic frame",* constitutes a permanent category, whereas the social category is made of *"the historical frame"* and *"the psychic frame"*. These two categories act permanently upon the social will so that, by reaction, they create economic, spiritual, political and legal values" (Bădina, O., 1966, p. 80).

Society is the product of "manifestations", where "economic and social values (science, art, religion) constitute the content of the existence of the social" (Gusti, D., 1932, p. 318), considered to be "constituting social categories". In order to maintain these two categories, other two social categories are necessary, destined to the organisation and ordering of facts and social life, which can determine and regulate the essence of the existence of human society, i.e. the legal and the political, called "regulating social categories".

The existence of the social was explained by professor D. Gusti "only through its constituting elements, i.e. the economic and the spiritual, and by the elements that order it, i.e. the legal and the political, structured in parallel as functions within the social entirety" (Gusti, D., 1968, p. 280).

Beside frames, which represent the process of birth and development of social life, and beside manifestations, which are the activities of social life, we must mention the issue of the existence of the social and of social processes. Man is part of numerous and various groups, being attracted, influenced and determined by the units of the social where he lives, thus a supra-individual world (made of economic, spiritual, legal and political values) along with the inter-individual world of social groups.

The reality of social units is based on phenomena of will. "Social will can be understood as a phenomenon, as a fact, something that has become, or as process, event, something that is becoming" (Gusti, D., 1919, p. 15, *apud* Bădina O., Neamțu, O., 1967, p. 215). Professor Gusti's conception is focused on the idea of will and its modality of existence.

Social will can be observed and characterised by reporting the manifestations: economic, spiritual, legal and political to the set of frames: cosmological, biologic, psychic and historic, which leads to the law of sociologic parallelism. The law of social parallelism "regulates the nature of relations among frames, manifestations and social will: they are relations of interdependency, coexistence and not of logical subordination" (Larionescu, M., 2007, p. 121). This treble parallelism is found: among extrasocial and social frames; among constituting and regulating manifestations; among frames and manifestations; "inside the frames, a parallelism among extrasocial, cosmological and biologic frames, on the one hand, and the social, psychic and historic frames, on the other hand; then a parallelism within the constituting manifestations – economic and spiritual, and regulating manifestations – political and legal; and last but not least, a parallelism among the set of manifestation and the set of frames" (Gusti, D., Herseni, T., Stahl, H.H., 1999, p. 9). Thus, we have a *treble parallelism* (Gusti, D., 1968, pp. 238 – 239): among extrasocial frames (cosmic and biologic) and social frames (psychic and historic); within manifestations, i.e. among the constituting frames (economic and spiritual) and the regulating or ordering frames (political and legal); and among the set of frames and manifestations. The evolution trends within the set of social units can be established based on the *sociologic parallelism*.

Social will (Gusti, D., 1968, p. 281) can be characterised by:

1. "research of parallelism of manifestation by sub-units, as well as by establishing the parallelism between manifestations and the circumstances of conditioned frames, for each of these sub-units;
2. identifying the types of correlations among manifestations, as well as the types of correlations among manifestations and frames;
3. determining the social distances among groups, their relations, and the way they are integrated into the social entirety."

Social reality is undergoing a process of permanent transformation, according to the imperatives of social ideal and the means of achieving social values. Their totality forms "the System of a global Social Science" with the purpose of fully knowing social reality.

According to professor Gusti's doctrine, social phenomena channelled towards achievements and purposes are manifestations of will focused on goal reaching. He claims that there are two distinct realities: one natural and one rational, the two being in fact social reality (Bădina, O., Neamțu, O., 1967, p. 183).

D. Gusti affirmed that "society is the synthetic totality of people who live together consciously and carry out will manifestations such as: an economic and a spiritual activity regulated from the ethic and legal point of view, and politically organised, and conditioned comically, biologically, psychically and historically" (Gusti, D., 1968, p. 47).

In his work "Monographic sociology – science of social reality" D. Gusti mentioned that the novelty of the sociologic system consisted in the "possibility offered by a system of sociology which, without prejudicing reality, assures it, on the contrary, a systematic and integral research" (Bădina, O., 1966, p. 81). The research must start by the analysis of "the frames of social units", studying "comic", "biologic"; "spiritual" and "historic" factors, followed by the recording of "economic, spiritual, political-administrative and legal manifestations", and thus enabling the determination of structural types by comparison of phenomena.

Dimitrie Gusti, under the influence of ideas and expertise acquired by systematic study, succeeded in creating a personal system of sociologic thinking, entitled "System of sociology, ethics and politics" (Figure 1.1. System of sociology, ethics and politics, source: Gusti, D., 1968, p. 237 – see Annex), a theoretic model lying at the basis of the field investigations performed by multidisciplinary teams.

In his work "Sozialwissenschaften, Soziologie, Ethik und Politik" he presented the relation between sociology, ethics and politics, the three fundamental sciences of social life, highlighting the differences in attitude and method, as well as their connection of mutual completion.

The three sciences support one another, forming a unitary system of conceiving social life, and thus to the "two attitudes of knowledge two fundamental social sciences correspond:

1. a science of fact finding and explanation, the science of social reality as it is found at present, i.e. sociology; and
2. a science of appreciation and valuing, the science of norms, of social life purposes and of moral ideal, the science of future social reality, of ideal societies, i.e. ethics. Between the present social reality, already achieved, and the future social reality, i.e. the ideal to reach, a third activity takes place, giving birth to a new category of scientific problems. The activity of transforming present social reality in accordance with the ethical idea, or the activity of achieving the social and ethical values and norms, the system of means constituting the object of another social science, i.e. politics" (Gusti, D., 1968, p. 371).

The principles guiding the monographic labour and the position of the Bucharest School.

The sociologic monograph monitors the facts of social reality in view of building scientific theoretic constructions, and the method used is observation. Professor D. Gusti affirmed: "The sociological monograph, as it is conceived by us, *is not a mere collection of facts.* It does not follow the facts for an interest *in se*, but attempts to build and ground on them theoretic considerations of science (…). We start from the conviction that any science is related to reality (…). Our endeavour goes precisely in that direction: to give theory, that is science, a sure ground in the very reality it is called to clarify and orient. That is why we defined sociology as science of social reality and we claim that the only method promoting human knowledge and awareness is *observation*" (Gusti, D. *et al.*, 1999, p. 51).

Observation is applied to certain categories of phenomena, systematically and according to well-set rules: "In our conception, the sociologic monograph deals with *concrete social units,* such as a village, a town, a region. (...) The choice of a one single concrete phenomenon gives the opportunity of a much more detailed research and thus with surer results. (...) Only grounded on monograph can the research about the spreading of a phenomenon lead to rich and serious scientific results" (Gusti, D. *et al.*, 1999, p. 52).

The social unit delimited in space comprises individuals organised "in a certain order of co-ordination or hierachisation and fulfils characteristic functions, which strengthen even more its individuality" and has a whole character. Gusti considered social unit as object of research, as follows: "The monographic sociology formulated as the science of social reality should start from the social unit, because social reality *in se* appears under the form of social units" (Gusti, D., 1999, p. 53).

The second characteristic of sociologic monographs is "nature and order of problems", that were exposed by professor D. Gusti as follows: "The social unit appears as a reality in itself, with specific features, with a distinct existence. That is why *the first sociological problem* in relation with it is the *analysis of its essence and structure.* The social units being in fact groups of people, their forms of life have will as essence. (...) The manifestations of will or the *social manifestations constitute the second essential problem of a realistic sociology.* A social unit, after being studied in its structure, should be studied in its manifestations. After having established the composition of a unit and its organisation, we must determine what functions it fulfils, what activities it performs and what its present appearance is. Our system of sociology attempts at typologically reducing social manifestations, and establishes their number at four: *economic, spiritual, legal and political.* This typology also confers an original character to the monographs we elaborate, as they, beside the study of social units, are also the study of social manifestations, (...) in all their concrete aspects. Will is not absolutely free it its manifestations. It depends on a *series of natural and social conditions,* which give social units, according to the place and time, various appearances. The geographic environment, race, historical past, mentality etc. also play an important part in people's fate and realist sociology cannot ignore them, so much as without them we cannot foresee a scientific explanation of social phenomena. As regards conditioning factors or social frames, as we call them, our system tries to reduce their typology and sets their type number at four: the *cosmological, biologic, historic and psychic* frame. Frames constitute *the third fundamental problem of field sociologic research,* according to the indications of reality itself and the critical discernment that makes us *distinguish the unit from its manifestations and the latter from the frame where they emerge."* The procedure of the Bucharest Sociology School, as professor Gusti used to say, *"takes into account nothing else but reality"* (Gusti, D. et al., 1999, pp. 54 – 55).

2. Monographic sociology– science of social reality

The monographic researches performed by the Bucharest Sociology School are collective works originating from a co-operation of sociology with other sciences. During the monographic campaigns, other specialists work along sociologists: jurists, psychologists, historians, geographers, economists, ethnographers, biologists etc., as they are willing to know together the characteristics of rural life and to improve their working methods.

Sociology is the science of social reality. Social reality is a complex system of parallel manifestations of social units, conditioned by natural and social frames and motivated by social will.

The social is described as being "the product of a spatial, temporal, vital and spiritual conjuncture" (Gusti, D., 1969, p. 116), i.e. the "extra-social" frames: cosmological, biologic; and the "social" frames: historic and psychological, whereas social activity gets concretised through four categories: economic and spiritual, as well as political and legal. The economic and spiritual categories, considered to be constituting social categories, cannot be maintained without the regulating social categories, i.e. the political and legal ones, which have the role to organise and order them.

The social exists through its constituting elements (the economic and the spiritual) and through the elements ordering it (the legal and the political), forming the social whole.

Beside the problem of frames (genesis of social life) and the problem of manifestations (activity of social life) we have to consider the problem of the phenomenological existence of the social under the form of units, relations among them that trigger social processes. The current observation shows that people belong to the most varied and numerous groups: family, religious or national community, economic, political, sports, sympathetic associations etc.

The individual lives in an individual world of economic, spiritual, legal and political values concomitantly with the individual world of social groupings.

The reality of social units is built on phenomena of will. The foundation of the existence of any unit is the affirmation of social will, as "the voluntary forces drive it, in relation with other units, so that in the end, through social processes we obtain the formation of increasingly complex and superior social units. Will is the essence of social life, and thus, according to the situation and action of social forces, social reality takes the form of equilibrium, opposition, sub-super-co-ordination, organisation" (Gusti, D., 1968, p. 281). Social will can be discovered and accurately characterised by comparing the economic, spiritual, political and legal manifestations with the set of cosmological, biologic, psychic and historical frames, constituting the law of sociological parallelism. There is a three-fold parallelism: within the frames (a parallelism among the extra-social frames: cosmological and biologic; and the social ones (psychological and historical), inside the manifestations (between the constitutive ones, economic and spiritual, as well as between the regulating ones (political and legal). Parallelism means mutual existential conditions. These categories do not form subordination relations and they cannot be reduced either to one another.

The evolution trends of social units can be established on the basis of the sociologic parallelism. Thus, social reality forms a totality of unitary life, having as motivation the social will conditioned by the four frames (cosmic, biologic, historic, psychic) and in parallel concretised in the four manifestations (spiritual, economic, political and legal).

The monographic method is the "direct observation of live reality with theoretic explanatory thoughts". The monograph means the selection of a well-determined social domain and its study through the "live method of observation". Observation aims at the personal study of the phenomenon in its reality. In order to observe one needs exercise, eye education, creation of a new sense that is the scientist's inner eye. Sociologic observation should by systematised and organised, and must respect the following rules (Gusti, D., 1968, pp. 239 – 249):

1. Observation must be *sincere, objective*. Scientific objectivity means the faithful rendering of reality, the presentation of facts without any addition from the part of the scientific observer, an impartial finding of facts.
2. Observation should be *exact and complete,* comprise all details in their variety, depths and unity. In the case of direct observation the lack of instruments should be replaced by the researcher's qualities. The art of conversation requires presence of spirit, ability to remove the timidity, fear, reluctance of the interviewed person. The sincere communication of the idea followed by research removes the distrust researcher faces during his visits "the fact that the monographer is hosted in village households is another means of friendly connection and at the same time a possibility of unhindered observation of the peasant's everyday life" (Gusti, D. *et al.*, 1999, p. 49). What is very important is the recording of the observed facts, their transcription on a separate chart for an easier scientific use.
3. Observation should be *controlled and verified,* obtaining the so-called "experimental" observation. It is necessary to resume observation, to apply confrontation and control by all the means in order to obtain the certainty of the narrated fact. The experimental reasoning consists in the verification of conclusions of a reasoning, starting from the observation, through the reasoning conclusions of a new observation. Thus, the two observations are mutually controlled.
4. The monographic observation should be *collective*. Social reality cannot be deciphered by a single specialised domain. In a system of sociology aiming at exhausting the study of social life (conditions of existence, life manifestations), collaboration of specialists is a fundamental requirement. In sociologic monographs, collective work is the

means to get a complete comprehension of the researched social reality.
5. In order to be scientific, observation should be *informed and prepared*. The monographic research is "work in a living social laboratory". That is why the researcher should be aware of all that was written about the respective locality and region, know the bibliography of the problem and must be endowed with the necessary technical instruments. The first condition for the success of the scientific researcher is his theoretical preparation. The scientific observation should respond to a problem or verify a previous hypothesis, thus a precise sense, and the researcher's impartiality is essential. "The observer cannot go in situ with any preconceived idea about the very state of the reality he is to research, but he cannot go either without a previous specialised preparation, meant to assure him the thoroughness of observation and scientific fruitfulness" (Gusti, D. et al., 1999, p. 52). The monographic researches conducted were based on professor D. Gusti's system of sociology: "The sociologic system, the work plans and questionnaires prepared in view of a systematic observation are verified in the field every moment and are maintained only to the extent of the truth they contain and the advantage they offer. The scientific observation is thus always active. (…) the members of our team did not rest on the conquered laurels and were not content with the first results, but they worked incessantly to the improvement of their working method, raising doubt to the rank of method, debating, criticising and contradicting, putting the dialectics of ideas together with the dialectics of facts, turning scientific experience into an experiment" (Gusti, D., 1968, p. 246).
6. The sociologic research must be *intuitive*. Observation is an act of creation, being a comprehension of the object and a framing of facts into a sociologic system. Sociology penetrates social reality, and thus we can speak about an objective intuition, as it reveals the sense and intimate nature of social phenomena, does not deform or modify social reality. The climax of monographic researches is the following: "thinking is objectified, the ego sees from its exterior into the inside of beings and things, understands and judges them, ignoring his own person and own sentiments, grasps the exact nature of things by a direct understanding, under the internal angle of an informed

sociologic spirit aware of the global and superior purpose of research" (Gusti, D., 1968, p. 320). The sociologic research is an active penetration into the being of society, a research of senses and a rendering of reality.

The researched phenomena should be compared to other phenomena. That is why, beside the observation rules, comparison has an important scientific role. In sociology each social unit corresponds to a synthesis of the analyses that form the object of a larger synthesis, reaching the representative synthesis of social reality. The progressive elimination of the particular and the preservation of the essential traits are the result of the comparative method. And we can state the, if "observation is the most important method by which the observer makes contact with reality, comparison is the most important method of processing and scientific use of observation facts". Sociology as science of social reality uses both observation and comparison, the former is the "permanent source of all scientific data" and the latter "is the path of their transformation into science" (Gusti, D., 1968, p. 247).

3. Sociologic monograph

Professor D. Gusti used to understand sociologic monograph as "a time and space synthesis of a corner of the earth; a global view meant to combine the traditions of the past, the present reality and the future opportunities" (Gusti, D., 1968, p. 248).

The representatives of the monographic school define the sociologic monograph a follows:

– The sociologic monograph has the scientific mission of knowing social reality: "it provides us with a sure means of integral and detailed knowledge of reality, without which sociology as science is not possible. Due to the system closely guiding monographic researches, they are fully fruitful. The monograph is not confined to description nor to the fact collection; it rises to the most daring scientific operations, ranging from the discovery of the conditions of social phenomenon production to the explanation of the mechanism of

operation and intuitive comprehension of the deep objective meaning it comprises" (Gusti, D. *et al.*, 1999, p. 54).
- "The sociologic monograph is a method that enables sociology to systematically collect concrete data in view of its reasonings. In order to collect these concrete facts, the sociologist makes direct contact with a society that he systematically observes, based on previously elaborated hypotheses" (Costa-Foru, 1945, p. 26).
- "The monographic researches are meant to enhance also the country's historical knowledge, in this new sociologic meaning" (Herseni T., 1939 – 1940, p. 395 *apud* Vedinaş, T., 2001, p. 41).
- Neamţu Octavian pointed out that for the Monographic School sociology is "an autonomous domain of research, integrating part of the system of social sciences, performed by professionals, institutionalised in institutes and institutions specialised in sociologic research" (Neamţu, O., 1970, p. 9).

Along Dimitrie Gusti, other scientists such as Henri H. Stahl, Traian Herseni, Mircea Vulcănescu, Octavian Neamţu, Anton Golopenţia etc., by their personal works "have completed the complex profile of the Bucharest Sociologic School. Beside the fact that it grounded directions of rural sociology, some with an important global impact, in the wider plane of Romanian and European culture it has fallen within the frame of a matrix raising the issue of revealing the social balance in the social units, i.e. in the concrete forms of human association" (Vedinaş, T., 2001, pp. 36 – 37)

In the research of the social phenomenon, the monographic method was inaugurated by the representatives of the French school, such as Frederic Le Play, who analysed the workers' family, confining however to the analysis of the budget, in order to improve their situation; Henry de Tourville, who elaborated the so-called "Social nomenclature", the nomenclature with 25 classes and 365 elements; Edmond Demolins, who used the classifying principle taking into account geographic criteria in order to explain society (D. Gusti, 1968, p. 71; op. cit., p. 417).

The monographic method opened for sociology the possibility to become an autonomous science among the other autonomous sciences. Sociology must reach theory through facts.

The monographic sociology combines theory and facts, the former constituting the content, whereas the latter gives the scientific form and structure: "The sociologic system helps us distinguish the conditions of social life from its manifestations, elements that are so often mixed up in the field researches. The geographic environment or the population's biological status do not constitute *per se* an object of sociologic preoccupations. However, as soon as they influence in a certain manner the social reality we intend to study, we are forced to take them into account. (…) from the sociology viewpoint, they are mere conditions helping us reconstitute facts and discover their genesis. Thus the frames draw our attention upon the difference between the two fundamental problems of science, finding of facts and their explanation. The study of frames completes, with explanatory elements, the descriptive material collected thorough the study of manifestations. It is the only way to build a complete science. Due to the law of sociologic parallelism, this system also attracts our attention on the necessity to distinguish each frame from its manifestation. The social reality cannot be exhausted any other way" (Gusti, D., 1968, p. 241).

D. Gusti affirmed: "The novelty of the monographic researches conducted by us does not consist in the direct contact with reality – such researches are practised in other areas at a large scale – , but rather in the possibilities offered by a system of sociology which, without bringing any prejudice to reality, on the contrary, ensures its systematic and complete examination" (Gusti, D., 1968, p. 242).

Thus we realised the merge of sociology with the monograph, the former obtains an orientation towards its accomplishment as science. Sociology is the science of social reality, but social reality must be examined directly and in depth, and this is achieved only through the monographic investigation.

The monograph is the thorough scientific study regarding a certain well-determined social domain through the method of direct observation. The sociologic monograph follows the facts in order to build and establish on their basis the theoretical consideration of science, and the method which "promotes human knowledge" is observation.

The sociologic monographs conceived by the Bucharest Sociologic School have the originality of letting nothing unstudied of what is significant within a social unit, and rigorously applies the system of sociology in the monographic research "as an actual work plan meant to eliminate the risk of confusion and to ensure the reaching of all relevant sides of social reality" (Gusti, D., 1968, p. 376). Their objects of study are the social units "and they study them in a systematic and even organic order, from their living conditions to their objective manifestations and inner structure. Thus they provide sociology not only with a complete collection of materials, but also with the rigorous rendering of reality in its unitary forms and the opportunity to pass from description to explanation, to accomplish itself as science, in the true sense of the word" (Gusti, D., 1999, p. 55).

A society will always be conditioned by frames and manifestations that coexist. In order to realise a synthetic perspective of the Romanian reality, the sociologic monographs should comprise a study of all frames and manifestations.

In the field the order of studying the problems is reversed. We start from the study of frames that "give the measure and expression of social will", then we study the manifestations "the unit develops" and in the end we study "the structure and social process, in order to be able to characterise the will" (Gusti, D. *et al.*, 1999, p. 55).

The detailed observation of the *cosmological frame* means, for instance, how the village is situated, how the territory (mountains, hills, waters etc); sub-territory (ores etc.), super territory (climate, fauna, flora etc) and the works (interventions, modifications) made by men (forestation, irrigation etc) condition and influence the life of the place. The biologic frame should comprise the study of the population (birth rate, nuptiality, death rate, migration), racial composition of the place, the study of the biology issues (food, hygiene etc.). The analysis of the *historic frame* contains the settlement and development of the locality, the customs of the land, the administrative past etc., whereas the analysis of the *psychic frame* studies "the spiritual life of the village" with personalities and conflicts between tradition and fashion, public opinion etc.

The thorough study of the social manifestations consists in the analysis of *economic manifestations* (agriculture, fruit tress, live stock breeding, peasant household, household budget etc.), of the *spiritual manifestations* (religious, moral, artistic and ideological), of , *legal manifestations* (penal statistics, the issue of heritage, local legal customs etc.) and of *political manifestations* (parties, administration etc.). The sociologic monographs should aim at the study of social units (family, nation, vicinity school, church, mayor's office etc.), of social relations (relations of vicinity, of friendship etc.), of social processes (the process of socialisation, of individualisation, of urbanisation, of differentiating etc,), and also we must study the trends in social evolution (development, stagnation etc.).

The work plan, the research procedures and techniques are rigorously set. Thus, in designing a sociologic monograph there are three main moments: preparation, field research and processing and use of the data scientifically collected. The preparation stage consists in consulting the literature and all the documents related to the location of the planned research. In the field one starts by the study of frames, then of manifestations and eventually "the structure and social process, in order to characterise the will" (Gusti, D. *et al*, 1999, p. 55).

In the monographic research conducted by the Bucharest Sociologic School the village was considered the social unit of Romanian society. The first issue studied was that related to frames. In relation with the cosmic frame the field researcher studies the following issues: the region, the surfaces belonging to the village, the village core, the form and inner structure of the settlements (the village activity). The biologic frame consists in studying the population quantitatively – the demographic research (the population's structure, evolution and migration) and qualitatively – race, heredity. The historic frame means the study of historical documents, tradition and the way of transmitting culture from one generation to the next, all that is old and new in the life of the village. The last frame is the psychic one, with its two interlaced and interdependent planes: the personal plane with the "individual spiritual phenomena" and the group plane, "the collective spiritual phenomena", the latter completing the research of the sociologic determinism: "the social facts are facts of conscience, and thus they always have a spiritual background" (Gusti, D., 1968, p. 427).

After having studied the frames, which offer a rich range of problems, we proceed by studying the social manifestations, consisting in the study of the economic and spiritual manifestations, which represent constituting categories, and the legal and political manifestations, that are regulating categories.

Thus they started by the study of the village economic life, according to the form comprising several elements: "the land, tools, cattle, cash". The core point is the farmers' household that must be studied thoroughly, comprising "the real estate and the movables", the inventory of the assets that form the wealth, the family labour, the way of organisation and exploitation, the household budget. In order to comprise the peasant economy (the household industry) it was necessary to identify the village crafts, the way trade is conducted, live stock breeding, forestry, fruit trees, apiculture etc. "the passage from the close economy to the capitalist economy, certainly one of the most interesting issues to study in today's village undergoing a true transformation" (Gusti, D., 1968, p. 431).

Within the spiritual manifestations they studied: "the tongue"; literacy; religious life; beliefs and magic practises; clothing, "the costumes according to seasons, work and holidays, age and social status (…)"; popular systems of philosophy (geographic, biologic knowledge, folkloric astronomy etc.); traditions for birth, wedding, funeral, holidays and festivals.

In the study of moral-legal manifestations in the monographic researches they started by elaborating the statistics related to property, marital status, criminality etc. The village moral life meant the study of the conduct norms, moral sentiments and conceptions. "We have thus to monitor the peasants' moral psychology, their moral philosophy, their social ethic norms, mores and vices, their life of virtue, of morality and of deviation, of immorality" (Gusti, D., 1968, p. 434). In this ordering category they studied the family legal status (marriage, status of women and legitimate and illegitimate children, adoption etc.), the problem of assets and the way of transferring them.

The political-administrative manifestations consisted in the monitoring of the peasant' political conceptions, general policy and local policy.

The next step after the completion of the sociologic monograph was the processing of results "in order to reach, by the inductive method, more and more comprising generalisations" (Gusti, D., 1968, p. 436). The sociologic maps were obtained by mapping the revealed social phenomena, they were compared to those obtained in other researches and grace to the comparative method "one can establish the typology of different social phenomena, structural types and types of evolution . (…) sociology can formulate social laws and theoretical explanations with general character, fulfilling thus completely its function as a science. Sociology draws up monographs not merely to archive them, but to reach with their help reality-grounded theories" (Gusti, D., 1968, p. 436).

Professor Dimitrie Gusti affirmed that "sociology is a science of facts and their observation". In the case of the work method (as previously presented), the first characteristic of the sociologic method is to regard facts via *direct observations*. *The theoretic preparation* of the observer about the place of the future study must be complete as he has to know the theoretic work plan in its smallest details. Observation should fall within the research plan, having a precise direction in order to answer the problem studied. *Sincerity and objectivity* to facts means the elimination of all prejudices for the success of the research. In order to penetrate deep into the observed phenomena (or things), observation should be *accurate*, and the grasping of all nuances makes it *complete*. For reasons of thoroughness it should be *double-checked and verified*, i.e. the observations should be resumed and confronted so that the fact observed be studied in depth, aiming also at the use of experimental reasoning (consisting in the verification of the conclusions of a reasoning, which takes as starting point an observation, by the reasoning conclusions of some new observations) (Gusti, D., 1968, pp. 438 – 450). The sociologic monograph merges "the spontaneous exterior observation of phenomena with the observation of provoked phenomena or the experiment, and the latter with the inner observation, either by participation, or by understanding, reaching thus a complex method rich in knowledge opportunities, arriving thus at a synthetic method" (Gusti, D., 1968, p. 446). Along with the other methods, social phenomena should be researched also from the statistic viewpoint. A characteristic of sociologic monographs is the *theoretic steadiness* and its application in the field, "the organic relation between theory and facts, between system and reality" (Gusti, D., 1968, p. 503), and the results can be at the basis of future reforms.

Another characteristic of the sociologic monograph is that of *collective method*. The collective character of monographic researches requires a high number of specialists grouped in teams under the leadership of a sociologist, who had the role of co-ordinating field work, as well as of the realisation of the final synthesis. Thus, teams of specialists were organised for each frame, manifestation, social unit, social process, as well as a statistic team. The statistic team was the first to arrive at the research location, in order to enable the other teams to operate, supplying economic statistic data and the population's census.

The composition of the nine work teams participating in a monographic campaign was the following (Gusti, D., 1968, pp. 390 – 391):

- *The cosmological team* – for the cosmic frame, the team was made of a geologist a geographer, an agrochemist, a botanist, a zoologist and a sociologist;
- *The biologic team* – the team for the biologic frame was made of an anthropologist, a demographer, a physician and a hygienist;
- *The historic team* – the team for the historic frame was made of a historian, a palaeographer and a social historian;
- *The psychological team* – within this team an experimental psychologist and a social psychologist co-operated;
- *The economic team* – for the research of the economic manifestations the team was made of a social economist, a forestry economist and an agricultural economist, as well as a specialist in home industry;
- *The spiritual team* – the team for the spiritual manifestations was made of sociologists who researched religion, art, magic, customs and rites, a musical folklorist, a literary folklorist and a linguist;
- *The ethic-legal team* – the moral-juridical team was made of a historian of law, a criminologist and an ethician;
- *The political-administrative team* – in the administrative-political team an administrative jurist and a political sociologist collaborated;
- *The team for social units, relations and processes* – the team for social units and processes was made of several sociologists according to the complexity of issues (5 – 6 sociologists), as well as technicians: photographers, film operators, sketch artists etc.

As regards the work of the teams involved in a monographic research, D. Gusti pointed out: "The sociologic monograph, by its character of collective endeavour, respects the labour division and the specialisation purposes, but at the same time unifies all its scientific efforts and renders them their true sense, of pursuit of the truth as conform as possible with the global social reality" (Gusti, D., 1968, p. 446).

Beside the methodological aspects of sociologic monograph as field monographic technique they used the system of charts, the list of informants by issues and the individualised informant chars, a high number of forms.

The system of charts was used by researchers during the monographic campaigns in order to put down all the useful information "precisely in situ". The elaboration of the list of informants by issues was drawn up since the beginning, according to the type of problem. These informants were selected from the village, recognised by the local community "for instance, the most skilled charmer, the best mourners, the most talented singers, the most experienced shepherds, the most skilled household heads, the wisest elders etc. Thus, the researcher goes directly to the informant needed" (Gusti, D., 1968, p. 447). The information collected may be contradictory, requiring further verification, or incomplete. For each piece of information put down the informant name was written, elaborating an informant chart. *"The informant chart"* comprises his identification data "we should put down the gender and age, because both mentality and social experience varies according to these criteria. We should also note the informant's marital status and the social category as factors differentiating opinions and interests"(Gusti, D., 1968, p. 447).

In the monographic technique one distinguished between "the opinion chart" where the informant's point of view related to a fact was noted, and the "finding of facts chart" with the reality discovered by the researcher about the same fact, both being necessary for the comprehension of social life.

Another category of charts that monitored the "social value of phenomena" were the dissemination chart with the number of cases, the frequency chart containing the frequency of the phenomena and the circulation chart with the source of the phenomenon, the influence of other social units upon the place and the manner of propagating the social phenomena.

The monograph technique also used a high number of forms enabling the researcher to focus on important issues, and the results could be compared. Such forms were used in the realisation of the census, the research of birth rate, nuptiality, death rate, health, family budgets etc., and consequently of phenomena that can be studied quantitatively. For the qualitative phenomena one used "the guides – work plans" acting in two planes: issues related to a phenomenon and observation of that phenomenon in situ.

A remarkable importance in the monographic research was granted to drawing (sketches concretised in woven materials, tools, maps etc.), photography (catching people, material aspects etc.), phonograms of language and music, and film (documentary films in the villages Drăguș, Cornova, Șanț).

As a member of the sociologic seminar, Mrs. Xenia Costa-Foru participated in the sociologic monographic campaigns between 1927 and 1931 in the villages of Nerej, Fundul-Moldovei, Drăguș, Runcu and Cornova, focusing on the study of family life "starting from a questionnaire improvised at Nerej in the field research, and each new application of this questionnaire in these Romanian villages made me complete, correct and match it with the original method of sociologic monograph created by this seminar" (Costa-Foru, X., 1945, p. 1). As a results of the vast documentation and field experience, Xenia Costa-Foru, in the paper "The monographic research of the family. Methodological contribution" describes the plan of sociologic research of family life. The method of the family sociologic research (Costa-Foru, X., 1945, p. 30 – 37) starts from the scientific documentation and the elaboration of work hypotheses followed by the family inclusion into the sociologic monograph, the definition of the concept of family and the elaboration of the work plan, This research plan comprises two stages: the first is made of two sections "the description of family life phenomena and standard units" (standard units mean the through study of a family), whereas the second stage is the "sociologic analysis of the processes characterising family", performed and interpreted on the basis of the descriptive material collected. The structure of the first stage, containing the two aforementioned sections, is the following (Costa-Foru, X., 1945, pp. 297 – 323):

Section I: Research of the family problems throughout the village:

A. Identifying the problems and place, and analysis where family is surveyed;
B. External environment acting on the concept and family life consisting in the study of frames: cosmic, biologic, historic, psychological, as well as the research of the village manifestation acting on family: spiritual, economic, legal, administrative-political;

C. Study of family forms throughout the village. In order to conduct the study of the family as working technique we used the family tree that is "an attempt of graphically plotting all the relatives that brings together a group of people, descendants of the same elders" (Costa-Foru, X., 1945, p. 62);
D. Individual relations within family life, focused on:
  1. Relations between spouses:
     – marriage: average marriage age; marriage motivation and purpose, realisation of marriage and its ceremonial; dwelling manners etc.;
     – de facto relationships;
     – spouses cohabitation;
     – divorce.
  2. Study of the relations between ascendants and descendants, i.e.:
     • relations between parents and their married children:
       – common dwelling;
       – mutual rights and obligations;
       – conflicts.
     • Relations between parents and children:
       – Birth rate – number of children; "the parents' desire to have a limited number of children or no children" (op. cit. p. 311);
       – rights and obligations between parents and children.
     • Relations between grandparents and grandchildren.
  3. Relations between collateral relatives;
  4. Relation with distant relatives.
E. Relations of the family group:
  1. inter-family relations;
  2. family's relations with society and institutions;
  3. family's relations with the individual.

Section II: Monographic study of several types of families, comprising:

A. Location of the studied case in the general ensemble of the village;
B. Description of the group: family frame and manifestations of the family group;
C. Family's relations: relations between the family members and the family's relation with the community and society.

The forwarded theoretic work plan starts from the definition of the family as "social unit" and allows the recording of all aspects of family life.

The vast material collected during the monographic campaigns, by methods, work technique and technical means, aims at understanding social life, not only at its description, and what is specific for the Bucharest Sociologic School is that all specialised researchers focus their efforts on the same material "this endeavour of critical analysis of the material and of explanation, from inside it, of the big theoretic lines that impose to our judgement, should be made by all those who have to elaborate a fragment, no matter how small, of the entire set of monographic issues" (Stahl, H.H., 2001, pp. 125 – 126)

At the basis of sociologic monographs conducted there lies the sociologic theory, with the research plan and analysis manner of collected data, "the sociologic monograph we forward is a method, at the same time descriptive and explanatory; it collects material in a systematic manner, with the purpose of solving the most general problems from science, and it has an integral and direct character, attempting at researching a social unit from all points of view, directly, in situ" (Gusti, D., 1965, p. 150). On the basis of the doctrine of Professor Dimitrie Gusti and under his guidance, the Bucharest Sociologic Seminar conducted, in 1925, at Goicea Mare, the first monographic researches.

Professor Dimitrie Gusti, synthesising the system of sociology, ethics and politics, affirmed: "what is characteristic to the Romanian sociologic monograph is the fact that it is at the same time a method and a system of sociologic thinking. (…) In short, our system of sociology states the following: 1. Society is made of social units, i.e. groups of people interrelated by an active organisation and spiritual interdependence. 2. The essence of society is social will. 3. Social will performs, as life manifestations: an economic and a spiritual activity regulated by a legal activity and a political activity. 4. Social will is conditioned in its manifestation by cosmic, biologic, psychic and historic factors. 5. The changes undergone by society in time through its activity and under the influence of conditioning factors are called social processes. 6. The development beginnings we can grasp in the present reality and thus we can foresee with a certain precision are called social tendencies. We can have three scientific attitudes before the social reality thus conceived, which allow the constitution of three branches of social sciences: sociology, ethics and politics" (Gusti, D., 1968, pp. 501 – 502).

Chapter II
Development stages of the Romanian Sociology School

"The Bucharest Sociologic School" or "The School of Monographic Sociology" or "The Romanian School of Sociology", as it was also called by H.H. Stahl (Larionescu, M., coord., 1996, p. 82), starts from the principles of the scientific and practical activities forwarded by Professor Dimitrie Gusti in his inaugural lecture given at the University of Yassy in 1910. On the 18th of March 1918, in Yassy, he founded "The Association for Social Study and Reform", which by statute was an association for the study and implementation of social reforms; the proposal of solutions for the realisation of social reform, based on studies; contribution to the masses' education; organisation of the seven sections by specialisations; publication of an organism of the association; presentation of social life realities in conferences, congresses, lectures, publications etc. On the 1st April 1919 the first issue of the "Archive for Social Science and Reform" is published, a press organism of the Association for the Social Study and Reform, published at the "Social Reform Editions" of Bucharest, that also published D. Gusti's programmatic study "Social reality, science and reform".

Along with the transfer of Professor D. Gusti to the Chair of sociology, ethics and politics within the Faculty of Letters of the University of Bucharest, the association also relocated, and the second Ordinary General Assembly of the Association for Social Study and Reform decided, on the 13th of February 1921, its transformation into the "Romanian Social Institute" (R.S.I.). The members of the R.S.I. Committee were: Chairman – D. Gusti; Vice-Chairmen – C. Botez, C. Buşilă; Secretary General – V. Madgearu; Financial officer – I.N. Glogoveanu; members: G. Cipăianu, C. Rădulescu-Motru, I. Răducanu, C.Em. Krupenski, G. Taşcă, G. Ionescu-Siseşti, A. Lazăr, M.T. Djuvara, A. Teodorescu, M. Manoilescu, M. Sanielevici; auditors: Al. Costin, D. Ioaniţescu, N. Ionescu. Furthermore, for each of the nine sections a chairman was elected, as follows: agricultural section – G. Cipăianu; financial section – I. Răducanu; commercial section – G. Trașcă; industrial section – C. Bușilă; legal section – C. Botez; administrative section – A. Teodorescu; section for social and demographic policy and hygiene – M. Sanielevici; cultural section – C. Rădulescu-Motru; section for political and social theory – D. Gusti.

In the RSI sections scientific and political personalities of the time were mobilised, who carried out activities on several planes: debates and elaboration of law drafts and cycles of conferences related to the contemporary issues, as well as civic education.

During his first years of activity at the University of Bucharest, Professor D. Gusti elaborated and refined "the system of sociology, ethics and politics", the scientific instrument used in the action of sociologic investigation by direct field research.

1. The stage of the Bucharest Sociologic School

The first stage of evolution of the Bucharest Sociologic School, that of organisation, is characterised by: diverse actions outside the university, not based on the sociologic knowledge of realities; the RSI provided the organisational frame for the sociologic actions and researches to follow; the elaboration of the system of sociology by Professor D. Gusti, which constitutes the theoretic basis for the research of Romanian reality.

On the opening of the RSI Reading Room, on the 5th of December 1921, D. Gusti, in his speech, said: "R.S.I. tends to be the present, clear and well-defined expression of the idea that the wellbeing and progress of our people depend on the update of its national energy by a good organisation, which means, first of all, 'the will and the conscience of the working method. That is why R.S.I. is a co-operation of ideas and wills and has as life principles: 1) research of the social issues in general and of the Romanian ones in particular, in 9 sections; 2) documentation of the issues to research (…); 3) organisation of public lectures about a topic at the core of the preoccupations of the public spirit" (Diaconu, M., 2000, p. 68). The rhetorical question asked by Professor Gusti was: "What is the purpose of the RSI Reading Room?", explaining that its purpose is scientific, aiming at opening new horizons and perspectives, its task being to facilitate "the politics of the compared method, applied in social sciences"; it provides "(...) the attentive observer the tools to get acquainted with the statistic, moral, diplomatic, economic, cultural, legal, legislative, military, financial materials without which one cannot forward an authorised and clear opinion about the matters of the time" (Diaconu, M., 2000, p. 69).

In this period RSI organised cycles of lectures on different topics, such as: "Romania's new Constitution"; "Women's rights in the future Constitution"; Minorities and the future Constitution"; "Individual, society and state in the future Constitution"; etc.

In the amphitheatre of the University Foundation "Carol I" of Bucharest, the first cycle of public lectures was opened, on the topic "Romania's New Constitution", lectures given in the period December 18th 1921 – May 28th 1922. A number of 23 lectures from the RSI conferences were published in 1922 in the volume "Romania's New Constitution and the new European constitutions".

The second cycle of public lectures organised by RSI took place in the period December 3rd 1922 – May 26th 1923, and the topic was "Doctrines of political parties", a number of 11 lectures were attended, of which 19 were published in the volume "Doctrines of politic parties".

In the period April – June 1923, during the meetings of the Sociology Seminar led by Professor D. Gusti, they debated, elaborated and drew up a "Programme for the organisation of university life", published in the "Archive for social science and reform" (Gusti, D., 1924, pp. 174 – 191). These cycles organised by RSI continued by the lectures given by the sections, part of them being published in the "Archive for social science and reform".

The third cycle of lectures started on the 9th of December and treated the topic "Foreign Politics". Its was organised by RSI in the amphitheatre of the University Foundation "Carol I" of Bucharest.

The second stage of development is between 1925 and 1934, and the dominant element is the research of social realities in the field; the Gustian sociology becomes "monographic sociology".

The lectures continued. In the period January 18th – May 24th 1925 the fourth cycle of public lectures took place, on the topic "Romania's social life after the war".

On the 21st of January 1925 they founded the "Section for feminine studies" (under the leadership of Chairman C. Botez) within RSI with the purpose of studying the problems of women and children: "(…) taken into consideration in the social frame where their life and productive activity takes place, as well as the issues of social policy related to the situation of women for the fulfilment of the needs or present life, of the women's participation in this life and the conceptions about the state" (RSI, 1927, p. 525).

Starting with the 8th of February 1925, within the Sociology Seminar led by Professor D. Gust and the assistant G. Vlădescu-Răcoasa, the preparation for the first field trip began. During 20 meetings they discussed and drew up the plans for frames and manifestations, and in the meeting of April 11th 1925 it was decided to conduct the sociologic research in the village of Goicea, Dolj county, and the journey was set for the 24th of April.

The first monographic campaign took place in the village of Goicea-Mare, in the period April 25th – May 1st 1925, led by Professor D. Gusti accompanied by his assistant and eight students, as well as the graduate Mircea Vulcănescu. After the research M. Vulcănescu wrote: "The investigation had – scientifically – a double purpose: a general one: 1) to verify, first or all, in contact with the living reality of social life, the value of the standard rural monograph plan elaborated at the Seminar, (…); and a special one: 2) second, to collaborate somehow with the monographer of that village, (…)" (Diaconu, M., 2000, p. 112). The sociologic seminar made a donation of 100 books on the occasion of the establishment of the village library, and Professor Gusti was awarded the diploma of honorary citizen of the Goicea – Mare commune (April 29th 1925). During the Seminar meetings, after the return to Bucharest, the vast material collected was discussed, together with the questionnaires applied etc.

D. Gusti announced in "Romanian Sociology" that "we celebrate fifteen years since I elaborated, together with several young collaborators, members of the Sociology Seminar of the University of Bucharest, the first rural sociology monograph. We set out then, in 1925, for Goicea – Mare, with the precise intuition that direct observation on which the field research is grounded will open a new era for the Romanian sociology. We were persuaded that the continuous quarrel among schools and currents, undermining the western sociology for half a century, could be replaced, at least in our country, by a new path, of collaboration and fruitful endeavour. Today we are entitled to affirm that we were not wrong. The Romanian sociology became a science of reality, which abandoned the bare library for the living contact with facts, for the uninterrupted investigation of life in its immediate and deep forms" (Gusti, D., 1939, No. 4 – 6).

The year 1926 started by the fifth cycle of public lectures. Between the 10th of January and the 30th of May, the conferences dealt with the general topic "Capitalism in social life". They were published in a collective volume and also in the "Archive for social science and reform".

The second monographic campaign was implemented in the village of Ruşeţu in Brăila county in the period 12th – 26th June 1926, reuniting a number of 16 monographers and a photographer. Small teams were constituted who studied a set of issues, and at night meetings were held for discussing the material and improving the technical procedures and their adaptation to the specificity of the studied phenomenon. H.H. Stahl took part in this campaign. A people's library was opened, and D. Gusti was declared honorary citizen of the Ruşeţu village. As a result of this campaign, 22 papers were filed in the library of the Sociology Seminar, as well as the notebooks with observations and notes.

In the amphitheatre of the University Foundation "Carol I" of Bucharest on the 9th of January 1927 the sixth cycles of public lectures was opened, organised by RSI on the topic "The city and the village", and a number of 21 lectures were given.

Created by the initiative of D. Gusti, on the 11th of June 1927 The Bucharest University Office began its activity. The functions of the Office were the study of the university life, career counselling and assistance, as well as co-ordination of academic life. In October they published "The student's guide. Vademecum academicum. 1927 – 1928" Bucharest, Ed. of the Cultural Foundation "Prince Carol", and in its "foreword" Professor D. Gusti wrote: "The university is meant to help, first of all, the formation, enrichment and ennoblement of society's structure by the cultivation of science. (…) The professor and the students, by their equality of aspirations, focused on the same cult of the Truth, are only gradually distinct, by the nature of their existence; the professor is a perpetual student, whereas the student is by definition a novice teacher. They are part of one and the same family (...)" (Diaconu, M., 2000, pp. 131 – 135).

The third monographic campaign took place in the period July 16th – August 16th 1927, in the village of Nerej, Putna county, with the objective of studying the old social structures of the Romanian village. For this monographic campaign the team was made of 41 participants, among whom H.H. Stahl, Xenia Costa-Foru, Traian Herseni. For the preparation of the campaign, two monographers were sent ahead. The campaign started by a reunion in which Professor D. Gusti talked about collective work by teams, and the theme was set: "systematic and multilateral investigation of all families and households, elaboration of the complex census of the entire village, door to door (...)" (Caraion, P., 1971, p. 80). The focus was placed in the research on the study of families and households "investigating the improvement and progress of agricultural life"; "it is important for a social reform to be accurately aware of the present situation and to indicate ways for the necessary immediate changes" (Herseni, T., 2007, p. 15).

A library was also opened in the village and objects specific to the location were collected for a future exhibition. After this campaign the first sociologic monograph was published, entitled "Nerej, un village d'une region archaique / Nerej, a village of an archaic region" (1939) in three volumes.

Between the 20th of November 1927 and the 3rd of June 1928 the seventh cycle of public lectures were given by the RSI on the topic "Politics of culture".

The fourth campaign of monographic research organised by the Sociology Seminar of the University of Bucharest took place in the Câmpulung county, *in the village of Fundul Moldovei* in the period July 10th – August 10th 1928, conducted by a number of 62 participants from the Sociology Seminar and also specialists from other fields, marking the beginning of the mass scientific activity. In the evocation of the Bucharest Sociologic School, this campaign was crucial, because Professor D. Gusti completed the theoretic plan and H.H. Stahl refined the working techniques. The questionnaire used in this research had a new form, the notebooks were given up and replaced by charts by thematic folders. The village library was opened, and the objects collected in the village were later on exhibited in two rooms of the

Sociology Seminar of the University of Bucharest. The Association of Monographers was founded, with D. Gusti as elected chairman, and M. Vulcănescu, H.H. Stahl, N. Cornățeanu and D. Prejbeanu acting as vice-presidents, and in 1929 the association became the RSI's Sociologic Section.

The activity of the 12 sections within the RSI during the first half of 1929 was deployed by debates on the general topic "Romanian issues within international life".

The fifth monographic campaign was organised in the village of Drăguș, Făgăraș county, between June 13th and August 16th 1929, with the participation of 89 members (university professors, alumni, a film operator, a photographer etc..) and 3 locals. The teams were organised by "frames", "manifestations" and "units", accurately observing the diagram of the Gustian sociologic system. The issues approached were researched to the least detail, the village library was founded, with 556 books, Professor D. Gusti was awarded the title of honorary citizen of the Drăguș village. The sociologic material collected was exhibited in the exhibition organised by the Bucharest Sociology Seminar, and an 80-photo catalogue was edited, illustrating the activity of the monographic research conducted in Drăguș (29.11.1929). In his speech at the exhibition opening festivity, Professor Gusti said: "(…) A method is justified by the results of its application. The processing of tens of thousands of charts, innumerable statistics, plans, diagrams, sketches, an immense documentary material, over 600 photographs only from the last monographic campaign, await publication. (…) Our studies taught us to understand the great sociologic truth that the village is the sanctuary where the Romanian people's manifestation of life, separated under ephemeral circumstances, took refuge and is preserved, that it is the summative type, the synthesis of our people, the microcosm of the Nation, that the village is the charge of a Romanian life in a tiny corner of humanity" (Diaconu, M., 2000, pp. 204 – 205). The film "Drăguș" was made, comprising the work techniques, the dances of the place, ceremonies etc., film presented in January 1932 at the National Theatre of Bucharest. Due to its success, the film "Drăguș", appreciated as scientific document of sociologic awareness and publicity, was demanded by the Pedagogic Museum of Paris and the Institute of Roman Languages in Berlin (in 1934). The monograph of the Drăguș village was not finalised, but many related studies were published: Vulcănescu M. "The Romanian village", in *Realitatea ilustrată* (Vulcănescu, M., 1929, pp. 3 – 11); Herseni T. "The monographic methods in sociology", in *Societatea de mâine* (Herseni, T., 1929. no. 16 – 17); Amzăr D.C. "Drăguș. Settlement and village labour" in *Poșta informativă* (Amzăr, D.C., 1929, pp. 21 – 22); etc.

The eighth cycle of public lectures, hosted by the amphitheatre of the "Carol I" Foundation organised by RSI was given in the period November 10th – June 1st 1930, on the topic "Contemporary political and social experience".

The sixth monographic campaign was conducted in the village of Runcu, Gorj county, in the period June 29th – August 18th 1930. A number of 67 participants collected a vast material: 1200 charts and 600 photographs. On the 12th of August they were visited by the university assistant professor Helmuth Klocke, accompanied by 12 students, from the University of Leipzig, who were eager to observe the activity of the Romanian monographers. Following this campaign many papers and works were elaborated and published.

The topic "Federalisation of the European States within the constructive internationalism" was debated and presented during the ninth cycle of lectures organised by RSI (beginning with November 16th 1930).

The village of Cornova in the Orhei county (Basarabia) was selected for the seventh monographic campaign organised by the Sociology Seminar of the University of Bucharest. It was realised in the period June 25th – August 13th 1931. The research was conducted by 55 participants, and the objective, the theory and the methodology of the research were similar to those of the last two campaigns (Drăguș – 1929 and Runcu – 1930). A Czech student, Kudrnovschi, actively participated in the entire campaign. A second sociologic film was made, a cultural home and a library were founded. In the first half of 1932, within the Sociology Sections of RSI, the participants' papers were presented from the material collected in the Cornova campaign, also published in the "Archive for social science and reform".

In the period January 13th – May 29th 1932 the tenth cycle of public lectures organised by RSI was given on the topic "Influence of world economic depression in Romania"; comprising 8 conferences.

In the summer of 1932 no new monographic campaign was organised, only a small team returned to Drăguş, three years after the first survey, to conduct a verification of the data collected in 1929 and to grasp the changes occurred. Furthermore, a small team returned to Drăguş in the summer of 1933 to perform reverifications in view of elaborating the materials for publication.

Traian Herseni described the monographic campaign as follows: "The realisation of a science ideal like that pursued by Professor Dimitrie Gusti requires a vast organisation of common labour, a numerous group of people to serve it with devotion (like any great fate, the monograph lives exclusively through its followers), a skilled, persistent and enthusiast leadership, a strong will before hardships, an unshaken conviction in the moments of doubt, a personality to stop trivialisation and superficiality, to give the impulse and to maintain the preoccupation at the height of the things completed for eternity, for truth, a great leader energy. We had them all in the person of our chairman, Professor D. Gusti, and of the most distinguished monographers" (Herseni, T., 1932, p. 573).

Professor D. Gusti was appointed, in the period August 11th 1932 – November 13th 1933, Minister of Education, Cults and Arts.

The second stage in the evolution of the Bucharest Sociologic School ends in 1934 by the publication of the volumes "Technique of sociologic monograph" by H.H. Stahl and "Theory of sociologic monograph" by T. Herseni, and the introductory study of Professor D.Gusti "Monographic sociology, science of social reality".

The third stage in the evolution of the Bucharest Sociologic School marks: "a) the fusion between sociologic knowledge and cultural action as state guided activity; b) promotion of sociology as "science of the nation", as well as c) affirmation of the Romanian sociology school on the international level" (Caraion, P., 1971, p. 87). In 1934, D. Gusti is appointed Director of the "Royal Cultural Foundation Prince Carol", and thus, beside the other public office positions, head of the Chair of Sociology, Ethics and Politics and Chairman of RSI, he could apply his conception in the field of social-cultural action in the village, and thus combine knowledge with action, in accordance with his doctrine.

Between 1934 and 1938, each summer the Foundation sent students' teams to the villages, and thus a number of 2563 team members carried out their activity in 114 villages situated in 57 counties for the action of "the village cultural awakening".

The monographic campaigns of 1935 and 1936, led by Professor D. Gusti, took place in the *village of Şanţ* (Năsăud county). The Şanţ campaigns were preceded by the activity of students' teams, which made monographers' work easier and showed their co-operation with students, and had the purpose of elaborating a "model monograph" for the following researches.

RSI published since 1936 the journal "Romanian Sociology" comprising the field monographic studies, and four years later the collection "Romania's Sociology" appears, with the first published monographs. The sociologic investigation conducted by Anton Golopenţia and Dr. D.C. Georgescu resulted in five volumes entitled "Sixty Romanian villages researched by the students' teams in the summer of 1938", of which four were published beginning with 1939 in the collection "Romania's Sociology". The work brings about a novelty, one passed from the complex monograph of a village to the study of the fundamental issues in several villages, using statistic and typological methods. The zonal (or regional) sociologic research conducted by Anton Golopenţia and Mihai Pop entitled "Dîmbovnic, a district in the south of the Argeş" was published only in 1942 (three years after the completion) in the journal "Romanian sociology". The synthesis study drawn up by D. Gusti, *Today's status of the Romanian village*, is the result of these inquiries, the issues approached being the economic situation, cultural and sanitary conditions, the author pointing out that: "The summary monograph of typical villages show the diversity of rural Romania. Our villages are not in the least identical" (Bădescu, I., Cucu-Oancea, O., 2005, p. 325).

In the same period, T. Herseni conducted the regional sociologic investigation in the Olt Country, using the typological methods, while a large team of specialists led by Professor D. Gusti were working on the "Romania's Encyclopaedia", made of thematically organised studies, according to the diagram of the Gustian sociologic system. "Romania's Encyclopaedia" started with the preface entitled "A synthesis of national economy; "Volumes I and II of Romania's Encyclopaedia refer to the political and administrative life of the Romanian State. Volumes III and IV regard economic life. Together with volumes V and VI, that are to be published and will be dedicated to Romanian culture, Romania's Encyclopaedia will put at readers' disposal a full picture of the accomplishment of the Romanian nation, as it appears for the conscience of their children, at the end of the second decade since the realisation of its political unity".

In 1936 the Museum of the Romanian Village is created and opened. In his speech, D. Gusti said "(…) this Village Museum is made of households brought from all the corners of the country in order to give a true image of the life of this category of our nation on whom we all rely (…)" (Gusti, D., 1965, p. 219). The Village Museum is the result of monographic campaigns in the Romanian villages. "Begun with the thought of limiting ourselves to the mere scientific research, we felt the need to collect objects from the village life" (Gusti, D., 1965, p. 223). The first step was the museum opened for the public in 1928, in the premises of the Bucharest Sociology Seminar, with the objects from the Nerej households and those collected from the campaign organised at Fundul Moldovei, and in 1929 "the fruit of researchers" in the Drăguş village (Făgăraş county) resulted in the exhibition hosted by an entire room dedicated to the village of Drăguş. The students' teams collected a rich material from the Romanian villages, at the urge of Professor D. Gusti: "Dear team mates, we invite you to put yourselves in the service of this idea, to co-operate with your effort and skills in the selection of the material to exhibit, to the realisation of the Museum of the Romanian Village. We would like that all your contributions should constitute not only the beginning, but also the strongest foundation of the future museum of Romanian villages" (Gusti, D., 1965, pp. 225 – 226). Professor D. Gusti said at the opening "(…) we hope to inspire especially the youth of our country, to see what could be accomplished by generations of students who have been working for ten years, steadily and silently, for the Romanian village, so that this museum could be an example of what can be accomplished by an endeavour taken to sacrifice, and to listen to our appeal to turn the work for the awakening of the village into a creed and a foundation for their entire life" (Gusti, D., 1965, p. 229).

In this stage also we can mention the Law of Social Service, passed on October 18th 1938 promulgated by his Majesty King Carol the Second, which had a great theoretical and practical importance for Romania's social life.

The initiator of the law for the establishment of the Social Service was Professor D. Gusti, also appointed the chairman of the institution, "with the rank and attributions of the Ministry of State" (Gusti, D., 1938, p. 398), who, since 1936, was asking for the introduction of the mandatory Social Service for any pedagogic school graduate.

Although the institution of the Social Service had a very brief existence, between October 1938 and October 1939, it constituted the most advanced stage of the fieldwork. The scientific, ethical and political value of Professor Gusti's accomplishments with the institution of the Social Service was appreciated by many sociologists, as well as by President Roosevelt, who considered it to be one of the most advanced laws adopted in the world at the time.

The law of the Social Service brought about an original contribution to the doctrine of scientific politics and stipulated the compulsoriness of a stage in the countryside for the graduates of the universities and higher institutions: "a young person who had graduated from a high school or a faculty was to be obliged by law to provide an educational labour in the countryside during 3 – 6 months, a cultural activity mandatory for the issue of his bachelor degree diploma" (Rostás Z., 2005, p. 43).

For the comprehension of the practical solutions adopted b the Law of Social Service it is necessary to present the data and general lines at the basis of the doctrine (Gusti, D., 1970, pp. 200 – 215):

I. The scientific doctrine of the Social Service:
   a) *Social reality and its study.* Society is made of economic, spiritual, legal and administrative-political manifestations, which in their turn are conditioned by a natural category – the cosmic and biologic frame – and a social category – the historical and psychic frame, thus a complex phenomenon that can be studied only by working in a multidisciplinary team. The analysis of the social units is done through direct monographic studies. By the study of increasingly complex social units we arrive at the study of the entire nation, and then at the "Science of Nations".

b) *The study of reality and the social ideal.* Following the study of social reality, the scientific conclusions obtained are doubled "by a social ideal".
c) *The social ideal and the political means of accomplishment.* The facts of social reality are an entirety with an independent structure and with its own social will, that is why any social reform should be complete on the ensemble of the forms of social life and of causes triggering it.

The scientific doctrine of the Social Service is based on the "affirmation of the necessity to study social reality, with the help of direct researches of the sociologic monographs, based on a just conception of human personality and on the research of the means of cultural place, able to turn a social unit into a single creation will" (Gusti, D., 1999, p. 92).

II. The previous experiences of the Law of Social Service:
   a) *The monographic surveys.* The great expansion of the campaigns of sociologic monographs in the Romanian villages is due to the co-operation of the Romanian Social Institute with the students of the University of Bucharest, which led to the formation of a practical and theoretical school, with academic character, and to the birth of the "Romanian School of Sociology".
   b) *The cultural homes* were organisations joined by the village intellectuals: priests, teachers, state authorities, representatives of the village. The motto of the Cultural Homes was *Health, Labour, Soul and Spirit,* in accordance with the four branches: protection of public health, labour organisation, moral and intellectual culture.
   c) *The Royal Students' Teams.* In 1934, out of the initiative of his Majesty King Carol the Second, the Students' Teams were created, made of students from different specialisations who, for 5 years, in the summer months, conducted investigations in the Romanian villages, being assisted and guided by official technicians of the State. Through the Royal foundation "Prince Carol" the teams experimented the best working methods for the Cultural Homes, following the doctrine of the School (formation of teams and working schedule), the result of the campaigns being numerous sociologic documentations.

III. *The Law of the Social Service* appears along with a pre-existing social movement and combines scientific research with practical constructive action.

The Social Service introduced the necessity of institutionalised actions i.e. by the establishment of Cultural Homes in each village and town, meant to offer organised social-cultural and economic actions. Thus, diverse sides of social life stipulated in the Law of Social Service were performed in the Cultural Home, and it was the unit of integration for social and administrative life, promoting the local trends of development or transformation (Neamţu, O., 1971, p. 154).

The Social Service had the following purposes (art.1):
- Preparation and guidance of graduates "in the labour of village reorganising, understood as a civic and national obligation;
- The creation, for this purpose, as execution organisms, of the Cultural Homes, meant to lead the village life (…);
- To organise and manage the endeavour of country knowledge, by monographic researches, which will constitute the foundation of the works of the Social Service;
- To organise schools for the education of villagers and town inhabitants, in view of the activity of Cultural Homes and schools for the training of the youth, called to the Social Service" (Marinescu, C., 1995, p. 23).

   a) *Romania's Institute of Social Researches.* Along with the coming into force of the law of Social Service the research activity of the Monographic School was restructured. Article 1, par. c, indicated the organisation of monographic committees with the purpose of "organising and leading the endeavour of country's knowledge by monographic researches, which will made the foundation of the works of Romania's Social Service" (Bădina O., 1966, pp. 88 – 89). Romania's Institute of Monographic Researches, part of the Social Service, had the role to organise "efforts of knowledge" of the country and comprised the institutes of regional researches, which centralised the county committees. Article 16 of the Law of Social Service transformed the former social institutes into institutes of regional social researches (in

Bucharest, Timișoara, Iași, Constanța etc.) subordinated to Romania's Social Institute, which becomes Romania's Institute of Social Researches with the role of "organising , leading and co-ordinating the works in all social domains dedicated to the scientific knowledge of the country and nation" (Gusti, D., 1938, pp. 573 – 574). The elaboration of the investigation plans and the synthesis of materials are the task of the Institute of Researches, made of 15 sections: social geography and natural riches; social biology and public health; culture; language; farming and co-operation; commerce, credit, currency; industrial; public finances; political and administrative sciences; journalism and propaganda; minorities and Romanians abroad; national defence; foreign politics, statistics; sociology.

b) *Extension of Cultural Homes.* In the period 1934 – 1938, their number became 2308, and then, within a year, another 1245 units were established, showing the cultural need of the country. The state authorities supported the social-cultural actions and institutions. By the activity of the cultural associations led by D. Gusti a new working method was defined and verified, i.e. "knowledge and action", in the mass cultural activity. (Neamțu, O., 1971, p.154).

c) *Extension of rural schools.* For the development of Cultural Homes, the Royal Foundation "Prince Carol" founded rural schools for the training of young peasants, where they were made aware of their duties to the state, and schools for the managers of Cultural Homes, for the intellectuals, where they were initiated in the methods of social investigations and in the aspirations of cultural policy.

There were many schools and training courses for villagers: "1. Rural courses organised by the Cultural Homes; 2. Rural schools organised by the County Cultural Homes, with the stakeholders from a county, for a set period, in boarding conditions; 3. Superior peasant schools for, organised in permanent specially endowed locations, in conditions of boarding school and with a schedule for two to three years" (Neamțu, O., 1971, pp. 156 – 157). The style and functioning structure of the superior peasant school was similar to the university although it was addressed to a public with low school training. As issues of contemporary interest were debated, we can say that the Superior Peasant School was an important accomplishment of the Social Service. For the top management of the Cultural Homes persons needed to be trained to know the methods of cultural labour and to build intellectual and moral capacity, prestige and social authority. Starting with 1935, from two courses one reached the number of 496 courses in 1939, attended by over 20000 trainees.

d) *The mandatory Social Service for the youth.* Article 5 of the Law for the establishment of the Social Service details the purpose and character of the Social Service, whereas article 8 shows that the instrument of accomplishment of the Social Service is represented by the Cultural Homes. Article 5 stipulated that the graduates of universities, of higher schools and institutions must provide the mandatory service in the villages. In order to fill a position, together with the diploma, the certificate of completion of the Social Service was required. D. Gusti's attempt to involve the youth in actions and activities with spiritual, social and political character was a success. In 1939 a number of 3210 young persons attended throughout the country, and participated in the noble action of village awakening and progress. "Our intellectuals should make contact with the social reality of the villages, which constitute 80% of Romania's settlements (...) for those who are destined to be part of the leading class of a country, it is extremely useful to complete a period of direct labour, of inquiry and social action among the peasants, as the sole means of knowing their suffering and greatness. Thus, due to the activity of teams, a new intellectuality is formed. From the professional viewpoint, our young intellectuals have the possibility to make the proof of their capacity of administrators and creators, as the tasks entrusted to them are precisely to profit from their brief stay in the villages, in order to leave there a mark of constructive humanity." (Gusti, D., 1999, p. 98). The intention was that the youth get aware of the social organisation, peasants' life, to help to the progress of villages acting as "social engineers". It was intended to shape social personalities able to master the social-cultural theory and practice, able to initiate collective activities for the transformation of the existing reality into a superior reality.

The commanding corps of the Social Service was made of former team members prepared in the special school created by Professor Gusti and his students in the period 1934 – 1938, which played an important part in the organisation of the activity of youth teams. The mission of the 248 commanding officials of the Social Service was to organise and lead the preparatory schools for the young people who had to comply with the stipulations of the law of Social Service. 31 schools were organised for the youth, called preparatory schools or camps for the Social Service of the Youth or S.S.T Camps, which functioned, in diverse centres of the country. In these schools the youth learned that by detailed monographic researches one can know and distinguish the real situation from the apparent one, and then, on this basis, a new social reality can be built. According to the Law and Regulation, after a month of training in camp schools, the graduates organised in teams went to 128 villages to complete the field work. The work of the teams in the countryside was interrupted 6 days after their installation, and in October 1939 the application of the law of the Social Service was suspended.

In the same period, the Bucharest Sociologic School obtained an international prestige, fact attested by the decision that the 14th International Congress of Sociology take place in Bucharest, in the period August – September 1939 (instead of New York), chaired by D. Gusti as president and by C. Gini as vice-president. Unfortunately the Congress was never held, because of the international political situation (Poland's attack by Hitler's Germany which started the Second World War).

The fourth stage (1940 – 1944) in the evolution of the Bucharest Sociologic School is predominantly theoretical. Works are edited for the support of foreign sociologists so that they can get acquainted with the doctrine and scientific activity of the Bucharest School: "Nerej, un village d'une region arhaique, monographie sociologique dirijee par H.H. Stahl / Nerej, a village of an archaic region, sociologic monograph conducted by H.H. Stahl, (3 vol.)"; "Clopotiva, a village in the Hațeg Country (2 vol.)" – monograph led by I. Conea; "Sixty Romanian villages" etc.

Beginning with 1933 Professor D. Gusti gave lectures abroad, and gained imposing authority on the international stage, due to the echo of the monographic activity in the country. He gave two conferences at Sorbonne (Paris, 1935) with the theme "La monographie et l'action monographique en Roumanie / The monograph and the monographic action in Romania", and at the International Congress of Sociology in Brussels (1935) he gave the lecture "La sociology des unites sociales / Sociology of social units". In 1937 the Professor's paper presented at the International Congress of Social Sciences was entitled "La Sociology et les Sciences Sociales / Sociology and Social Sciences", and at the International Congress of Sociology he presented the paper "La loi du parallelisme sociologique comme loi d'equilibre social / The law of sociologic parallelism as law of social balance". The lectures continued at the universities of Munich and Berlin, and in Leipzig he was awarded the title of "doctor rerum politicarum honoris causa". On June 24th 1939, on the occasion of his election as corespondent member of the "Academie des sciences Morales et Politiques de l' Institut de France / The academy of moral and political sciences of the Institute of France" he presents the paper "Law of the Social Service in Romania".

The activity carried on by the monographic school had an important impact upon foreign specialists, the Romanian sociologic conception was made known also in the USA grace to the articles of Philip E. Mosely such as "The Sociological School of Dimitrie Gusti" (April 1936) and "A new Romanian Journal of Rural Sociology" (1937). In 1935, the American specialist Philip E. Mosely participated in the research conducted in the village of Șanț, Năsăud county, and he affirmed that: "D. Gusti is the creator of a unitary sociologic system, the organiser of a unique school of field activity and the inspirer of an increasing movement of improvement of the village situation. Despite the financial difficulties, he succeeded in fulfilling the task he set for himself. His personal dynamism is felt everywhere, both in the administrative field, and in the field of local activity, in the channelling of the tiny resources he has at disposal, raising the enthusiasm of intellectuals and peasants by his idealism and determination" (Mosely, P.E., 1936, p. 165). The scientific fame of the Bucharest Sociologic School increased and attracted many foreign researchers and students. Moreover, in the period 1946 – 1947, Professor Gusti gave lectures in France at the "Academie des Sciences Morale et Politiques / Academy of Moral and Political Sciences" of Paris, as well at universities in the United States: Yale, Harvard, Wisconsin (lecture followed by the preparation of the sociologic film made in the Șanț village), Chicago (the paper entitled "An Approach to the Study of Social Reality" that was to be published in the "American Journal of Sociology") (Gusti, D., 1970, pp. 283 – 301).

The monographic campaigns "organised and conducted by D. Gusti took place between the years 1925 – 1946, studying 626 villages, towns and regions, proving a priority interest for the research of the village as social unit *in se* (in inter-war Romania there were over 15000 villages)" (Otovescu, D., (coord.), 2006, p. 128). The statistic of researches is the following: 626 villages, towns and regions, organisation of 5000 cultural homes and over 500 rural schools, the purpose of these researches being the coverage of the entirety, leading in the end to a sociology of the nation. RSI, by its two-decade activity, can be described as "an institution that researched the fundamental issues that preoccupied the life of inter-war Romania, which contributed, simultaneously, to the promotion of the cultural relations with the foreign countries, especially of European solidarity, so necessary then as it is today" (Larionescu, M., 2007, p. 390).

The defining dimensions by which the Romanian Sociology School, initiated and organised by Professor Dimitrie Gusti, is imposed as "original social phenomenon" are the following (Stahl, H.H., 1980, pp. 10 – 12, *apud* Bălan, C.C., 2001, p. 54):

- "It created and applied a new method of research for the social realities, i.e. by interdisciplinary teams established since 1925;
- It initiated on the national scale an application of this method of interdisciplinary research, by direct and systematic contact with local realities, with the final confessed purpose of elaborating "a sociology of the nation";

- It aimed at a practical goal of social-political nature – establishment of the technique of social action, that can enable the reaching of immediate goals, animated by high ideals of social ethics;
- The scientific character was doubled by a cultural movement of direct action, fruitful in experiment procedures of scientific involvement in the effective march of society towards the reaching of higher social-cultural levels".

2. Superior School of Social Work

The first school of social work in Romania was the Superior School of Social Work and Assistance "Princess Ileana", established on the 1st of November 1929 in Bucharest. The idea of establishing such a school started from the Association of Christian Women of Romania and was realised under the aegis of the Romania Social Institute, the president of SRI, Professor D. Gusti, supporting its organisation. In 1949 "The Superior School of Social Work and Assistance "Princess Ileana" became "The Institute of Social Work" then in 1951 it was turned into the "Institute of Social Services Providing". The latter was transformed into a post-secondary education system on the 11th of September and was functional until 1969.

D. Gusti considered that the social problems could not be solved only by charity actions, the intervention of social assistance was necessary, and the issued had "to be studied by a scientific social assistance". Social work and assistance, according to the conception of Professor Dimitrie Gusti, in the vision of the Bucharest Sociologic School, was considered a specialised branch of sociology, the purpose being the formulation of social policies in view of solving the phenomena of social deviance. The desiderata of scientific social assistance and work were:

1. "To allow the knowledge of problems and 'worrying' situations of social life. Such problems were represented by disorganised families, prostitutes, beggars, vagrants, criminals, under age delinquents etc., for whom it was necessary not only to organise units of social protection (nurseries, day centres, orphanages, retirement homes, re-education colonies), but also to develop direct actions from case to

case. These problems were to be identified by the technique of sociologic monographs, realised both in villages and in towns.
2. To elaborate techniques of direct intervention, individualised for cases similar to those presented above, realising in this hypostasis, an open social assistance" (Stănoiu, A., Voinea, M., 1983, pp. 48 – 49).

The first director of the Superior School of Social Work and Assistance in Romania was Mrs. Veturia Manuilă, and the patronage committee comprised His Royal Highness Princess Ileana – president; Professor Iuliu Moldovan – Secretary General, the delegate of the Ministry of Health and Social Assistance; Professor Dimitrie Gusti – chairman of the Romanian Social Institute; Mrs. Frederique Romalo – Chairman of the Association of Christian Association of Romania.

The teaching staff was made of the personalities recruited by V. Manuilă: Dr. Xenia Costa-Foru, Henri H. Stahl, Mircea Vulcănescu, Traian Herseni, E. Bucuţa, Dr. Sabin Manuilă, C. Nichita, A. Pavel, Dr. N. Romanescu etc.

The apparition and development of the Romanian school of social work and assistance was initiated and supported by this strong group, being a direct product of the preoccupations of the Bucharest Sociologic School: "assimilating the peak experience in the USA and Europe, they imprinted a strongly original orientation, possible due to the huge effort of sociologic research developed in Romania. The strong principle option of social work developed in Romania of that period was, on the one hand, its massive grounding on the sociologic research of social problems to be approached , and on the other hand the active involvement in the units of social protection" (Zamfir, E., 1999, p. 240).

The school organisation plan was drawn up by Professors Iuliu Moldovan and Constanţa Georgescu (representative of the Association of Christian Women of Romania). Iuliu Moldovan considered that "social work is one of the important factors of psychic and moral prosperity of a people" (Mănoiu, F., Epureanu, V., 1996, p. 131).

Through the curricula and syllabi elaborated under the guidance of Professor D. Gusti one aimed at acquiring knowledge from the domains: sociology, psychology, economy, law, as well as knowledge related to the problems of social life. The objectives of the curriculum were focused on:

a) "Awareness of the great issues of urban social life, both theoretically, by the critical presentation of the literature, and by the analysis of the situations specific to our country. It comprised courses of lectures in family bio-sociology (normal, disorganised, de facto relationships, divorcees), the sociology of community and socially dependent social groups, of delinquency, social inadaptation, problems of women and children.
b) General information necessary for any social activist, regarding the country legislation, political economy, sociology, general and differential psychology, hygiene and public health etc.
c) Method and technique of social investigations, general and for case studies; vital and social statistics, accounting.
d) Techniques of social action by communities and groups or regarding individual social cases; organisation of units and institutions of social protection.

In accordance with these courses, the specialised practical training was organised, in experimental centres structured as follows:

1. For the family assistance – Demonstration centre in the Tei district, where they attempted the elaboration of a district monograph, initially started in 1930 by the taking over of the tasks to organise here the state census.
2. For the hospital social services – Demonstration centre hosted by the Colțea Hospital.
3. For the practice in industrial assistance – the A.C.F.R. organisation
4. Then the practise centres were multiplied by adding state institutions such as The Minors Tribunal of Bucharest and the Văcărești prison, the Colentina Hospital – nervous diseases ward and venereal diseases ward for the individualised assistance of prostitutes, and the Central Hospital of mental and nervous diseases, for the psychiatric assistance; the Filantropia Hospital for the heart diseases and maternity ward. Specialised wards were also organised at the hospitals Pantelimon, Brâncovenesc, dr. Cantacuzino etc.
5. For the assistance of the children – centres at the Society St. Ecaterina Orphanage, the Society Prince Mircea and the children hospital. The activities were extended in the country, by creating centres of social

assistance at the protection offices at the municipalities of Braşov, Cluj, Sibiu, Craiova, Ploieşti, Timişoara." (Stahl, H.H., 1980, pp. 341 – 342 *apud* Zamfir, E., 1999, pp. 241 – 242).

Until 1959 the curriculum for social workers was of 4 years, and the specialised practice was guided and organised within the Romanian Social Institute. Moreover, Elena Zamfir stated the importance of the relation between education and practical side "What can be appreciated for the social assistance education by D. Gusti's Sociologic School is the close connection between social theory and its practically-applied side" (Zamfir, E., 2004, pp. 16 – 17).

The Superior School of Social Work and Assistance collaborated with the Seminar of the Faculty of Philosophy – Sociology Section – using the scientific data from the monographic results, with RSI, which organised in 1932 a cycle of conferences to disseminate its purpose. There was a good co-operation with the Central Institute of Statistics and with the Association for the Progress of Social Assistance, established along with the graduation of the first alumni of social assistance, which hosted the library organised by the Superior School of Social Assistance and the Central Institute of Statistics. Under the leadership of Mrs. Xenia Costa-Foru, who was part of the monographic team, the students from the school of social assistance helped to the performance of social inquiries: "According Stahl's testimony, the school of social assistance had become the most efficient supplier of social investigators for Gusti's sociologists" (Rostás, Z., 2005, p. 72), and they participated in the Cornova and Fibiş campaigns.

In order to get acquainted with the mode of statistic data analysis, the students of the Superior School of Social Work and Assistance attended the practical training at the Central Institute of Statistics, acquiring also the knowledge about the problems requiring intervention. In 1936 the section of social statistics (established at the initiative of Professor Gusti) conducted the first census in the domain of the social work problems in the country, identifying a number of "521 units of social assistance, of which 50 state units and 471 private associations" (Mănoiu, F., Epureanu, V., 1996, p. 6). The results of the census of units and the actions of social work actions were published in the volume "Institutions of Social Work and Protection". Moreover, with the support of Professor Dimitrie Gusti one organised in 1938 the first Congress of Social Workers in Romania.

The Superior School had a period of development, with multiple collaborations, established the publication "Social Work" that was also called "The Bulletin of the Superior School of Social Work and Assistance Princess Ileana" (in the period 1929 – 1936), where they presented the actions of social work, its connections with other institutes in the country and abroad, published studies and researches in the field of family assistance, assistance of the minor delinquents etc. Beginning with 1936, the year of the establishment of the Association for the Progress of Social Work, under the leadership of D. Gusti, it also took over the Journal of Social Assistance, publication that appeared twice a year until 1944. This Association, the organism maintaining the connection between the specialists in the country, aimed at creating a close relation between the theory and practice of social work and assistance.

As regards the mission of social assistance, Dimitrie Gusti affirmed that "social assistance exceeded the trenches of generous sentimentalism and of mere good intentions, in order to step into the field of an ordered and thoroughly motivated social and ethical action with the exclusive purpose of serving society not through books and theory, but through the finding of the social truth among the hard conflicts of life" (Mănoiu, F., Epureanu, V., 1996, p. 1).

Chapter III
The Banat-Crişana Social Institute – promoter and innovator of the research ideas and methods initiated by the Bucharest Sociologic School

1. Constitution and organisation of the Banat – Crişana Social Institute

Dimitrie Gusti's work and creation marked a new era in the organisation of sociology from an interdisciplinary perspective and in direct relation with practice and social life.

The scientific and cultural movement developed under the leadership of Professor Dimitrie Gusti for the investigation of social reality triggered the creation of several institutions more or less independent to the Romanian Social Institute, all inspired form his activity and supported scientifically and morally by him.

The Banat-Crişana Social Institute (B.C.S.I.) was founded on the 21st of May 1932, in Timişoara, by a group of intellectuals, grouped around Timişoara's Mayor Cornel Grofşorean, who had become aware of the necessity of investigating social reality in Banat. Since the beginning two personalities came forward who showed an interest for the sociologic study, i.e. Dr. Cornel Grofşorean, who had studied in Budapest and had preoccupations in the field of social research, and dr. Iosif Nemoianu who, grace to studies of social medicine, drew the attention of Professor Dimitrie Gusti. The idea of creating the institute came in 1929, on the occasion of a Congress of Yugoslavia refugees, when it was remarked that Romanian did not have a documentation centre about the Romanians living in the neighbouring countries. A future institute could compensate this absence in the regional plane, and research Banat's complex issues, which, as C. Grofşorean put it, could be solved only on the basis of a scientific study, conducted by a scientific institution (Grofşorean, C., 1932, f. 2 – 4).

A first step was made in the autumn of 1931, along with the adhesion of the Professors' Board of the Polytechnic School for the creation of an institute of social researches.

The conference focused on the issues of creating a social institute in Timişoara took place on the 7th of February 1932, when they defined the landmarks of the future activities (Grofşorean, C., 1938, p. 125, *apud* Bălan, C.C. 2004, p. 21): "to know social realities in the Banat-Crişana region in order to persuade the authorities, the entitled organisms and the entire country about the true situations in these regions, to stimulate the political thinking in order to prepare the citizens for a civic conscious life".

Mr. C. Grofşorean was designated as the person to establish the official contacts with the chairman of the Bucharest Social Institute, Professor D. Gusti. Since the beginning the Timişoara representatives decided the autonomy of the institute in relation with the Bucharest Social Institute, fact accepted by the chairman Dimitrie Gusti.

The idea of creating the Banat social institute preoccupied also Iosif Nemoianu who, according to his confession of 1942, reached the conclusion that "we will not be able to govern the new provinces unless we perform, first of all, their inventory in all aspects" (Nemoianu, I., 1942, p. 283).

The entire group was convinced that in this way it would be possible to inventory the problems of Banat in the historical context after 1918 and to formulate several strategies: "constituted for national and spiritual imperative, with the declared purpose to perform the scientific grounding of social action (…); the appeal to the knowledge by the research of social realities is made in view of identifying the means of solving the deficiencies identified and the grounding of a viable policies for the region where it functions" (Bălan, C.C., 2001, p. 95).

There were other reasons also: the social research and action of the BCSI supposed a close connection with the administrative authorities "in direct contact with the administrative authorities, with the purpose to inform the state authorities about the social status, so that these authorities, using the scientific findings, could take the necessary measures." (Nemoianu, I., 1942, p. 295); the defence of the western frontier through study; necessity to know the problems of Banat minorities "the Banat model of interethnic integration"; of the situation of the Romanians living abroad, of the Romanian communities living in other countries.

Furthermore, the institute should also be connected to the sentiment of frustration the Banat inhabitants were experiencing due to the fact that there was no university in Timişoara, like in other cities of the country. The university was to contribute to the Banat and Timişoara cultural prestige, to provide the frame for a scientific activity of Banat intellectuals.

Thus, the model of the Bucharest Sociologic School inspired the creation of the Banat Crişana Social Institute, not only structurally, but also methodologically, the Banat inhabitants becoming aware of the importance of an enhanced knowledge, prior to any action of economic, social, cultural, agricultural or political reform.

On the 21st of May 1932, in a festive context organised at the Prefecture of the Timiş-Torontal county, with the participation of the founding members, of the delegation from Bucharest and the city notabilities, the Banat-Crişana Social Institute was officially created, with the central office in Timişoara and an autonomous and independent branch in Arad. Professor D. Gusti, in his speech, reminded the history and accomplishments of R.S.I. as well as the importance of the research issues and the dissemination of results, urging action and wishing the BCSI "to start with the same modesty and boldness we had, and, as the social science is a science of observation, supposing first of all a sovereign mastering, either through experience or though culture of facts – and less by inspiration, in your activity you should keep in mind that you have the responsibility of a methodical documentation on all problems of social and political life in this corner of the country, that will offer you a vast field of scientific documentation" (Gusti, D., 1933, p. 33).

The statute approved by the constituting assembly contained: name, central office and purpose; means; organisation; activity; and the members of the institute. The structure of the board of directors, according to the Statute of the BCSI was:

− Chairman: V. Blaşianu, Rector of the Timişoara Polytechnic School;
− Vice-president: C. Grofşorean (Banat), C. Radu (Crişana);
− Secretary General: Iosif Nemoianu;

- Presidents of the sections: eng. Dion Mardan, att. Adrian Brudariu, dr. Ioachim Miloia, eng. Victor Vlad, dr. Mihai Gropşianu, dr. Cornel Grofşorean, dr. Virgil Popovici.

At the constitution meeting the statutes were approved, drawn up according to the model of the RSI, by which the Institute forwards its purpose in Art. 1 (BCSI., 1933, p. 35):

a) "to research the issues of social sciences regarding to the social status of the region along the western frontier";
b) to procure for its members or any other person interested in such issues the scientific studies and papers conducted and elaborated by its sections;
c) To contribute to the dissemination of the social, folkloric, artistic, technical knowledge and literary studies without any lucrative purpose".

In order to reach these goals, the following means were necessary:

a) "the activity of the members grouped by specialisation's;
b) organising publications;
c) granting awards;
d) organising survey and inquiries;
e) spreading the knowledge about social issues by conferences, congresses, publications, lectures and field trips;
f) the establishment of: 1. One library containing Romanian and foreign publications about social matters; 2. An archive with information materials of any nature. 3. An information office. 4. A statistic office" (BCSI., 1933, p. 35).

The premises for the central office were acquired on the 27th of November 1932, and the Ministry of Justice acknowledges the Banat Crişana Social Institute as legal person on the 2nd of December 1932.

Compared to the RSI organisational structure, BCSI had seven sections (two sections less), renouncing to the section of political and social theory, its attributions being taken over by the section of social policy and sociology; on the other hand one created the minority section, necessary for the analysis of the situation of Banat minorities, and the grouping of specialists in the established sections was different. Thus, the chairmen of the sections were:

- eng. Dion Mardan (economic, financial, technical, farming section);
- att. Adrian Brudariu (social policy and sociology section);
- dr. Ioachim Miloia (cultural-artistic section);
- eng. Victor Vlad (urban and administrative studies section);
- dr. Mihai Gropşianu (legal-administrative section);
- dr. Cornel Grofşorean (minorities section);
- dr. Virgil Popovici (medical-sanitary section).

In the beginning the sections had a small number of members, but their number increased while the BCSI acquired prestige and authority. In the BCSI structure, along with the university staff, we find intellectuals from diverse domains, important personalities from the administrative organisms "we can consider that the intellectuals reunited within the BCSI represent '*social personalities*' – in the sense given to the concept by D. Gusti (Bădescu, *et al.,* 1996, p. 629) – combining "the four great dominants and characteristics that form a four-fold voluntarism: 1. The will to be what you are (…). 2. The will to participate in social life (…). 3. The will to create social and cultural values within the nation (…). 4. The will to persevere in the reaching of social and national goals, with courage and spirit of sacrifice, in the sense of the three aforementioned purposes" (Bălan, C.C. 2001, p. 93).

In the first year of activity, according to the Secretary General's Report (March 31st 1934), the sections had 265 members, and the structure of the sections was the following:

- social politics and sociology – 51 members;
- medical-sanitary – 29 members;
- cultural and artistic – 56 members;
- urban and administrative – 21 members;
- minorities – 33 members;
- economy, finances, technics, farming – 26 members.

We remark the absence of the juridical section, its attributions being taken over, in the beginning, by the Banat Legal Circle, and only in 1935 the BCSI established its own legal section by the adhesion of 27 persons (Negru, A., 1999, p. 57).

In its first period of existence, the activity of the institute consisted in the organisation of the sections, for which one established the goals, the priority issues, and the theoretic and methodology frame of approach and active intervention.

The relation between BCSI and RSI was special since the very beginning. The BCSI members declared themselves followers of the monographic school led by I. D. Gusti. However, as the conformism was not absolute, the autonomy referred to the way of applying the method, the manner of organising campaigns, the purposes pursued or the data processing (Grofşorean, 1938, p. 10). They all agreed that the reaching of the set goals could be accomplished only within a frame excluding external decisions.

From the viewpoint of the method, scientific competency and team activities, the RSI was regarded as a higher forum, but from the organisational perspective, the relations were not of subordination, a matter clarified since the beginning between C. Grofşorean and D. Gusti. The relations established by BCSI, through C. Grofşorean, with RSI and with Professor D. Gusti exceeded the strictly scientific sphere. Whenever there were difficulties in the activity, C. Grofşorean resorted to D.Gusti "Gusti never imposed anyone the strict application of his diagram. This is fully true in the case of all institutes (…).Gusti's guidance was manifested by the personal contacts he had with the leaders of the Banat institution" (Constantinescu, M., *et al,* 1974, p. 94).

Starting from the theoretic foundation of monographic researches (Gusti, D., 1968, p. 371) we should mention the distinction, but also the relationship among the three fundamental sciences of social life, i.e. sociology, ethics and politics. Social reality can be studied (the object of sociology is the present social reality) or appreciated in relation with the ethic ideal (the social ideal gives the appreciation criterion of social reality). Sociology identifies and explains the present social reality, whereas ethics is the science of norms, of social life purposes, of future social reality (of the ideal to reach). The relation between the present social reality and the future social reality requires a system of means brought about by another social science, politics. The three sciences support one another and thus "the complete study of social reality comprises three scientific domains:

- sociology: finding of facts and explanation of the present social reality;
- ethics: establishing the purposes of social life and of the moral ideal; and
- politics: researching the means meant to accomplish the social purposes and the moral ideal" (Gusti, D., 1968, p. 371).

The BCSI took from the Gustian methodology the stages of sociologic investigations: "establishment of the objet and purpose of the problem to study, and only then the proper preparation of the monograph; an important part is played here by the rules of observation, techniques of recording social facts, technique of processing the sociologic material and the typologies that were *rather explanatory, of proper empirical research"* (Bălan, C.C., 2001, p. 141).

In the Journal of BCSI (1933) the sociology section published a methodology material entitled "The Guide" which contained "the diagram of all issued and methodologies" (Bălan, C.C., 2001, p. 142).

The Institute carried on researches in a scientific system integrated in the Gustian method with certain deviations, setting only one process unit at a time and attempting at evaluating the structure, stage and development mechanisms of such a unit. Compared to the usual monographic diagram, the BCSI research brought a new element, that of investigating one single issue "the focus on a certain problem integrated in a more or less global description of the life of the respective unit" (Bălan, C.C., 2001, p. 9).

Henri H. Stahl affirmed in his work *Methodological and technical lessons* that "in fact the monographic research was focused, since the beginning, on *issues*, for a long period of time, tending to totally exhausting all problems existing in a certain limited social unit" (Stahl, H.H., 1971, p. 87). This type of research was possible in the development of the monographic researches accomplished by the Bucharest School as there was the potential of such investigations, compared to BCSI. Within the School a turning point occurred in the methodology when one concluded the importance of identifying the development trends or the social dysfunctionalities, and "one reached the conclusion that for the awareness of our social realities, it was not really the global image of certain villages or regions that was of the utmost interest, but rather the identification of the essential problems, that accounted for most effects, either in order to signal some critical sides of social life, or in order to grasp the development trends for certain social processes under way" (Stahl, H.H., 1971, p. 88).

In the "Annual Report" of May 31st 1934, the BCSI board justified the deviation from the research method of social reality practised by RSI as follows: "Our special circumstances – lack of tradition, of material means, of personnel familiarised with field sociologic investigation and the impossibility for the members of the Institute to go for longer periods in the villages, prevented us from following, as it would be only natural, the monographic method practised with such success by the RSI of Bucharest. That is why we had to adopt another way (…) the focus on the investigation of the most important and urgent problems of Banat" (BCSI, 31 March 1934).

A close observation of the monographic campaign conducted by the BCSI shows that the teams did not limit their focus on a certain problem, on the contrary, the research contains the complete analysis of the social unit, proving thus the appreciation of the Institute for the Monographic School led by Professor D. Gusti.

In this context, the Belinț and Sârbova campaigns aimed at researching the phenomenon of depopulation, but the research comprises both the study of frames and the study of manifestations, using the principles and the methodology of the Bucharest School. Thus, in order to comprehend the social reality, they analysed the economic and spiritual manifestations (with constitutive character) as well as the legal and political manifestation (with regulating character) that are conditioned by the cosmological, biologic, historic and psychological frames. Botiș E. pointed out that "both in Sârbova and in Belinț, consistent with the monographic method of Professor Dimitrie Gusti, we examined the villages investigation in its entire sociologic aspect, so that, from the set of the peasant's life manifestations in the investigated village we could identify the causes of the phenomenon of population drop, because we did not elaborate monographs focused only on the depopulation phenomena, but village or rural monographs" (Botiș, E., 1942a, p. 4).

Another determining element of the activity of the Institute in the pre-monographic period was the delivery of conferences and lectures in the rural areas. The first section that started the series of lectures was the medical-sanitary section, approaching diverse topics in its ten conferences. Nemoianu, who remarked himself through the lectures related to the issue of children, was also the first to inform the institute about the depopulation phenomenon. Furthermore, the cultural-artistic section had an intense activity grace to its ten conferences on topics from history, ethnography, education, arts, whereas the minorities section gave three lectures, one of them addressing the phenomenon of depopulation, i.e. the lecture given by E. Mihaiu entitled "The decrease of Banat population – period 1900 – 1930" (BCSI, 1933, pp. 81 – 83).

The priority issue of the BCSI in the first years was the very phenomenon of depopulation. "The conference of Mr. Sabin Manoilă, held in Timişoara and grounded on the data from the latest population census brought to the knowledge of public opinion a very sad finding: "Banat is depopulating". Grace to the existence of the Banat-Crişana Social Institute, this signal will not remain without echo, a mere word uttered in the desert; this sad warning is received and urges to action the small but soulful team of the Institute members. First of all it is crucial to research the cause of this danger, as the statistics of the general census are limited only to the sad finding that the death rate exceeds by far the birth rate, but does not comprise clarifying indications" (Bălan, C.C., 2001, p. 23). Considering it to be the most serious social phenomena, the leaders of the Institute presented the sections a project comprising over 100 topics related to this social-demographic phenomenon, and the Institute set its own programmes of activity for the year 1934. We can list in this respect (BCSI, 1934, pp. 85 – 90):

- The section of social policy and sociology: marriage and divorce, de facto marriages; social causes and effects of family abandonment; protection and assistance of the large families; family and labour; villages depopulation and its national and social consequences; birth rate in Banat by nationalities; birth rate policy; morals; modernism and family etc.;
- The cultural section: morals and birth rate in Banat; church and school; role of parents in the youth education and training for

marriage; Christian morality and birth rate, with applications about Banat; the single child type from the pedagogic and moral perspective etc.;
- The medical-social section: birth rate in the medical-social light; death rate; infant death rate; general death rate; role of TB in Banat depopulation; role of syphilis and venereal diseases in Banat depopulation; role of alcoholism in Banat depopulation; hygienic conditions of Banat peasants and depopulation; abortion and birth control methods etc.;
- The legal section: abortion and birth rate; marriage and birth rate in Banat; early age concubinage; research of paternity and birth rate; wealth communities and birth rate, contribution of the legislator to the promotion of birth rate in Banat etc.;
- The economic, financial, technical and agricultural section: revaluing of the social because of the village depopulation; Banat colonisation; intensive and modern culture of land; cereals; sale of farming produce etc.;
- The administrative and urban section: material assistance of the sick; the assistance of large families, the problem of dwellings in the villages and cities in relation with birth rate, fight against public immorality by administrative measures etc.;
- The minorities section: mutual influences between the Banat Romanians and minorities; the Suabians from the economic, cultural and moral perspective, the Hungarians from the economic, cultural and moral viewpoint; the Gypsies from the economic, cultural, moral perspective etc.;
- The statistic office: birth rate and death rate in Banat; infant general death rate; death rate and birth rate among diverse nationalities in Banat etc.

We may remark that the phenomenon of the Banat depopulation is researched by the sections of the Institute, and the Committee established as the core problem for the following two years, "the research of the Banat phenomenon – depopulation". This is precisely what happened, the first two researches of the BCSI took place in Belinț in 1934, and the second in Sârbova in the year 1935. The following campaigns were focused on other topics and were conducted in Pojejena (1936) and Ohaba-Bistra (1937).

In the period 1934 – 1939, along with the deployment of the monographic campaigns the series of conferences also continued, but their number was reduced compared to the pervious period. Thus, five conferences were held in 1934, seven in 1935, and only three conferences in 1936 and seven conferences in 1937.

The section of social policy and sociology that also had the role of co-ordinator of the results of the other sections' investigations, decided the establishment of a feminine section, with the purpose of integrating women in social activity: "the modern social problems cannot be solved in an advantageous manner without the contribution of the sensitivity, power of creation and practical sense that Romanian women prove brilliantly in the specifically feminine domains of action" (BCSI, 1935, no. 117). Furthermore, one established also the subsection of home industry, co-ordinated by Mrs. E. Secoşan, who set an ambitious programme of investigating and studying the creations in the Banat region, the collection of woven materials and authentic sewings in the area, the organisation of exhibitions and contests of folklore costumes etc. The activity of the section had its climactic moment at the 1939 exhibition of home industry, where one exhibited the materials collected from 38 rural localities, comprising five Banat's ethnographic areas, because "the affirmation of our national ethnicity is a vital necessity, when our attention is drawn towards the life of peasants in the villages, we should focus our attention and reach out to our home industry, which symbolises the exceptional artistic conceptions and is the most brilliant testimony of our autochthonous genius" (Secoşan, E., 1938, p. 134).

Along with the coming into force of the Law of Social Service (October 18th 1938), BCSI lost its autonomy and legal personality and operated under the name of the *Institute of Romania's Social Researches. Timişoara Regional Branch*, and the circuit of the Regional branch comprised the counties Timiş, Torontal, Caraş, Severin, Arad and Hunedoara. According to the Regulation (Art. 2), the purpose of the Regional Branch was (Bălan, C.C. 2001, p. 221):

– "To scientifically research the social reality in its region.
– To conduct monographic investigations and surveys.

- To put at the disposal of scientific institutions, authorities and its members the use of the studies, informative, statistic and documentary materials acquired as a result of its activity.
- To put at the Centre's disposal all the materials collected and processed by its team members and its sections.
- To contribute to the spreading of social knowledge by publications, public lectures or conferences".

Moreover, the researches of the Regional Branch are conducted in accordance with the method and work plans established by the Central Institute. The Regional branch can develop other scientific activities (beside those required by the Centre), examining the problems in the area, but have the obligation to inform the higher authorities and transmit the results of researches, the list of the participants and the activity of the sections.

The reorganisation of the sections was performed with the purpose of making easier the triage of the material collected by the teams, as they have the obligation to contribute to the knowledge of the country. Thus, the sections of the regional branch (Bălan, C.C., 2001, p. 222) were:

- "The geographic section,
- The biologic section,
- The historic section,
- The religious section,
- The cultural section,
- The economic and social section (farming and co-operation, commercial, financial and industrial),
- The legal section, with the subsection political and administrative sciences,
- The urbanism and ruralism section,
- The section for minorities and the Romanians living abroad".

Thus, all the institutes in the country "are turned into institutes of social researches in Bucharest, Yassy, Cernăuți, Timișoara, Constanța, Chișinău etc. and are subordinated to the Social Institute of Romania that, according to art. 16 of the Law of Social Service, became the Romania's Institute of Social Researches" (Bădina, O., 1965, p. 160). The role of this Institute was to "organise, lead and control the activities in all social domains dedicated to the scientific knowledge of the country and the nation" (Gusti, D., 1938, pp. 573 – 574).

Within the frame of the programme of the Social Service organised in the summer of 1939, the BCSI members participate in the Almăj Valley research, according to the schedule and using the work instruments received from the Centre, but the manner of observation and data collection was preserved, as they affirmed: "The Social Service adopted indirectly the finalist system of the social researches practised by us when it imposed us to research the communes in the Bozovici district, Caraş county in view of turning this unit into a model district" (Botiş, E., 1942b, p. 315, *apud* Bălan, C.C., 2001, p. 44).

After one year, the interruption of the activity of the Social Service (October 13th 1939) imposed the reorganisation of the Institute from Timişoara, so that on the 20th of May 1940 the Banat Crişana Social Institute was recreated, "with distinct legal personality", and the elect chairman was attorney-at-law PhD Cornel Grofşorean, the mentor of this Institute. The sections are restructured, and the new sections are: ethic-legal; agriculture; historic; folkloric; ethnographic and ethnologic (BCSI, 1944, f.11).

In the period 1940 – 1941 in the absence of the field researches the materials from the monographic campaigns are processed, and lectures and conference are organised in the limited circle of the members (I BCSI, 1941, pp. 272 – 274). Because of the lack of funds, in 1941 they organised only a one-day trip to Ghiroda (May 18th) more precisely in the Ghiroda camp, sheltering Romanians from the Timoc, in order to study the problems of the Romanians across the border, and the material gathered was published in the BCSI Journal.

In the summer of 1942, the monographic team members go to Naidăş in a last attempt to organise researches. In the two weeks spent there, the monographers conducted researches about the musical folklore, literature and costumes.

In the period 1943 – 1944, the internal activity of the sections was intense, the best example being the newly established historic section, which worked at the elaboration of the material destined to Romania's delegation at the future peace conference "in view of proving the anciety of the Romanian population on Banat territory and consequently of the necessity to maintain the existing state frontiers" (Negru, A., 1999, p. 84).

In 1945, because of the lack of funds, the BCSI suspended its activity, and in 1946, with the support of the Ministry of Agriculture and Domains they succeeded in printing the Journal of the Banat-Crişana Social Institute. The Journal of the Institute was published in the period 1933 – 1946 at Timişoara. A total of 98 issues were published, grouped in 37 volumes. The themes of the papers published in the journal and the scientific manner of presentation drew the attention of the local and national cultural-scientific circles.

The BCSI monographers did not limit themselves to researches, they carried out a cultural action materialised by the public conferences held in Timişoara, approaching problems of great importance exposed in an academic manner, in accordance with the prestige of this institute. Lectures were given by D. Gusti, Gh. Filipescu, A. Contrea, V. Popovici, Alex. Nicolescu, I. Nemoianu, A. Brudariu etc. The village conferences offered a first contact with the peasant masses and with the sad truths of their life, contact that was completed by the field investigations, and thus the peasant-intellectual, village-city relation was consolidated. Furthermore, in the manner of the Gustian school, during the monographic campaigns one organised social, cultural, educational, medical actions for the members of the respective community.

The stages completed by the BCSI during its 14 years of existence and scientific activity, in relation with the RSI, were of collaboration-association-integration. In the first period BCSI as autonomous Institute collaborated with RSI, and Professor D. Gusti was a real support for its activities. The stage of association corresponds to the year 1938, the year of the Ohaba-Bistra campaign, where the BCSI, the Royal Cultural Foundations "King Carol" and Astra united their forces in order to investigate the Romanian village.

The integration stage took place in 1938 along with the coming into force of the Law of Social Service, when the BCSI's independence ceased, and it was subordinated to the Romania's Institute of Social Researches and subsided by it.

Grace to the endeavours of its members, BCSI "responded since the beginning to a real necessity: knowing this region, its past, its present, the situation of the Romanian peasant from all points of view; collecting the scientific documents about his psychic, ethnic, social manifestations, in a word painting the real image of the Banat region, in order to find in the depth of documents guarantees and hopes for the future, as well as the means for improving the future" (Botiş, E., 1942a, pp. 1 – 2).

Chapter IV
The Banat-Crişana Social Institute monographic campaigns

The six monographic campaigns conducted in Banat proved the competency, rigour and professionalism of the BCSI teams, who investigated a number of 21 localities, and drew up an impressive number of charts. Focused on a certain problem considered of high interest for Banat, but analysing also the frames and manifestations in order to perform a deep analysis of the social phenomenon, the monographs are similar to those elaborated by R.S.I.

The Belinţ and Sârbova campaigns were finalised by the publication of the monographs, and the other campaigns provided ample studies published in the BCSI Journal.

Grace to the issues approached by the BCSI in the monographic campaigns: Banat depopulation, slow denationalisation of the Romanian elements, urbanisation, folk culture etc, it reached the set goals although the intervention of the authorities was reduced: "The viewpoint of the Institute was since the beginning the research of our villages' social reality in order to inform the relevant decision makers about the social realities, providing, beside well-defined conclusions, the necessary guidelines under the form of proposals. It is not our fault if the authorities have not always complied with our suggestions" (Botiş, E., 1942, *apud* Bălan, C.C., 2001, p. 123).

1. The Belinţ campaign

The series of monographic researches conducted by BCSI started with the *Belinţ campaign between August 15th – September 2nd 1934*. This commune was chosen because the phenomenon of depopulation manifested itself most poignantly in this village. This monographic investigation aimed at identifying the causes of depopulation.

As C.C. Teodorescu, chairman of the BCSI, affirmed in the preface to the volume "Monographic inquiry in the commune of Belinţ", the research fell within the sociologic preoccupations initiated by RSI, adopting the monographic method of Professor D. Gusti: "his monographic method was taken as foundation by us, and served as a frame where this research developed" (BCSI, 1938, p. III). The BCSI monographic team conducted a research in the commune of Belinţ studying and describing the frames and manifestations in order to clarify the causes of depopulation.

In order to clarify the phenomenon of depopulation it was necessary to get acquainted with the social reality. It is only based on these studies that one can take measures to fight against this "social plague" because "by this knowledge one reaches more easily to the grasping of the multiple causes that provoke it, or, in the worst scenario, one can determine the circumstances that support it" (BCSI, 1938, p. 6).

It was affirmed that the depopulation of the Romanians in Banat is founded on the model "ein Kind System" (one-child system) or "keine Kinder System" (no-children system) of the Germans colonised in Banat. The ulterior documentation revealed that this model was manifested among the Hungarian population before the Suabians. Kerek M. affirmed that this system with only one child was common among the Hungarian population of protestant faith, and it contaminated the other nationalities, and thus "in the period 1800 – 1840 this tradition was spread among the Saxons and Suabians in the south of Banat; between 1870 – 1880 this epidemic is manifest in Banat, contaminating the Serbians and the Suabians. Around 1890 – 1900 the system is spread also in the Caraş-Severin county, contaminating the Romanian population".

The statistic data of this study shows the influence of the economic crisis upon depopulation in the Hungarian plains. The author, Kerek M., pointed out that "it was not only the economic factor that triggered this defection, manifested even in the wealthy families, but fierce egotism, softening idleness and especially women's vanity have a high influence over the spreading of the system" (BCSI, 1938, pp. 330 – 331).

If it were only about a social imitation, the situation would not have been so serious. It was discovered that the phenomenon among the Banat Romanians, unlike the Germans, had two major causes: the first was the impeding of births and the second, excessive infant death rate , which led to the conclusion of an "endemic social plague". In order to efficiently fight against it was necessary to have a deep knowledge of the social reality in Belinț.

The method used was the inquiry or survey, with the application of the questionnaire instrument, according to the methodology of the Bucharest school, completed also with data resulted from the direct, individual or collective observations realised on the basis of charts. These were methods used preponderantly when the researched topic imposed the collection of small, but very numerous pieces of information, such as those referring to the lifestyle of the investigated persons. They analysed official documents, documentary sources, the church register of the dead, demographic movement of the population of the commune 1902 – 1933, the school archive for 1755 – 1933, the documents of the Recaș Court, works of musical folklore etc.

The monographic teams who participated, in the summer of 1934, in the Belinț campaign, were made of: 7 physicians (I. Nemoianu, I. Popa, M. Popovici, A. Maior, V. Popovici, N. Drăgan, I. Pruneș), 6 professors (T. Topliceanu, etc.), one teacher, 3 engineers, the director of the Museum of History, the head of the horticultural department, personnel with secondary education: "our investigators are not students, but autonomous professionals, specialised in their professions: physicians, professors, teachers, lawyers, engineers, agronomists, priests etc., i.e. people acquainted with social realities, in direct and perpetual contact with practical life" (BCSI, 1938, p. 2). Furthermore, at the request of C. Grofșorean, who demanded support from Bucharest for this campaign, O. Neamțu was appointed, who not only supervised the activity, but got directly involved, clarifying the importance of the use of family charts, economic charts and questionnaires.

The content of the monograph elaborated by the BCSI "The monographic inquiry in the commune of Belinț", was published in 1938, at the "Romanian Printing House of Timișoara", and the construction of the monographs followed the diagram of "frames" and "manifestations" elaborated by Dimitrie Gusti.

The volume contains the *general report on the findings of facts and improvement solutions proposed by the BCSI,* drawn up by professor Traian Topliceanu, as well as 22 reports forwarded by the five sections and the statistic office, and their proposals for the remedy of the deficiencies encountered.

The first reports analysed the frames and elaborated the geographic report (prof. A. Contrea), analysing the location of the commune, the relief, the climate, hydrologic network, vegetation, as well as the human factor; the historic report drawn up by I. Mioia presented the history of Belinț since its first documentary attesting; the first statistic report on the population in general, by prof. Emil Mihaiu, containing:

1. The statistic of the population (BCSI, 1938, pp. 36 – 60):
   - The population of the commune in the period 1869 (3473 inhabitants) – 1934 (1996 inhabitants), i.e. in 65 years, dropped by 43%;
   - According to the mother's tongue: Romanian is, for 95.3% of the population "the language in which man thinks and always uses in the bosom of his family" (BCSI, 1938, p.40), the commune is "all Romanian";
   - According to religion, in the year 1930 95.6% are Orthodox;
   - The population according to gender in the year 1934 is the following: 53.3% women and 46.7% men;
   - According to "literacy", a percentage of 58.5% could read and write.
2. The dynamics of the Belinț population:
   - Birth rate in 1931 was 15.8‰ (33 new born children), whereas in 1934 it was 12.9‰ (only 24 infants born in a year); the birth rate in the commune is very low (half) compared to the average birth rate of rural population throughout the country, which was 36.4‰ in 1931;
   - Death rate in 1931 was 29.3‰, it dropped to 24.8‰ in the year 1932, and then it increased again to 28.7‰ in 1934; for the year 1931 the average of the death rate coefficient of the rural population in the country was 21.6‰, value lower that that recorded in Belinț.

The depopulation of the Belinț commune is due to the low birth rate and the very high general death rate, but the "true causes of Banat's depopulation are different, i.e. economic, social, moral and hygienic in nature. Until our peasant does not acquire deeper knowledge about the importance of social hygiene, he will not be able to take care of the salvation of his health. Considering that populations' morbidity is increasing, the State, through its organisms, grace to free medical consultations and by putting at their disposal the medication needed must sacrifice themselves in order to heal the rural people" (BCSI, 1938, p. 59).

The second statistic report presents the conclusions regarding property, farming produce, taxes, consumption of strong alcohol, smoking, consumption of sugar, oil etc.

The medical-social section presented several reports:

1. *Report on the "infantile population"* by Dr. I. Nemoianu where findings of facts are presented related to the children's health and hygienic and social condition; using individual charts (following the model used by the Timişoara Centre for the protection of children), a number of 427 children were examined (of the total 431) aged between 0 and 15, according to the following criteria: medical, hygienic, social and psychic examination; one also applied intelligence tests, group verbal test, according to the Model of the Cluj Institute of Psychology.
2. *Report on the population's examination from the viewpoint of the "venereal diseases and sexual life"* by Dr. August Maior; he examined 592 men and 17 women based in a medical chart, with the afferent tests, and without charts, tests were performed in another 110 cases (93 women). As for the sexual life, a more advanced precocity was remarked compared to the urban environment.
3. *Report on the TB morbidity and death rate* was elaborated by Dr. I. Popa; he examined 1074 inhabitants aged over 15. In the period 1902 – 1912 a high death rate was recorded caused by TB "in 1908 the death rate was as high as 10%, a monstrous figure exceeding any other TB death rate known up to the present" (BCSI, 1938, p. 102); it decreased to 3.6% in the period 1922 – 1933. The problem identified was that the TB patients live in the same room with the rest of the family, as the dwelling is a source of propagation for the TB infection "first of all the most important part is played by the dwelling factor. Peasants do not possess the least elementary hygienic knowledge, they

live in the most primitive hygiene conditions, most dwellings are paved with earth, unaired, dusty, mostly deprived of sun and light. Beside the high crowd of people occupying them, they are the most favourable nests for Chronic TB. All the hygienic problems have, naturally, very noxious effects on the individuals' physical development" (BCSI, 1938, p. 115).

4. *Report on the medical-social investigation among women* drawn up by Dr. M. Popovici, who examined 703 women (of the total 850) from the somatic viewpoint, in order to sketch the anatomic-physiologic profile of the Belinţ female peasant.
5. *Report on the population's examination from the oculist perspective* realised by Dr. V. Popoviciu, who examined 1500 persons based on the medical-social charts;
6. *Report on the population's examination from the dentistry viewpoint* drawn up by Dr. N. Drăgan, who examined the denture of 1023 persons, finding the population's ignorance related to the oral.
7. *Report on the population's examination from the perspective of age, emigration, immigration and household hygiene,* by Gh. Atanasiu , who performed a demographic statistic: by age groups, as well as immigrations "took place only in the capacity of daughters-in-law or sons-in-law and contributed a lot to the maintenance of the population" and the emigrations that were very few, whereas about the home hygiene he pointed out that "it does not meet the required conditions" (BCSI, 1938, p. 184).

The cultural section forwarded three reports:

1. *Report on the religious life* by M. Bucătură, finding two opposed mentalities in Belinţ, one traditional and one modern, taken from the frequent contact with the city. "There are thus in Belinţ two social processes: 1. The process of tradition's preservation; 2. The process of urbanisation. These processes can be explained only by two mystic-religious mentalities of those who still live strongly under the pressure of the inherited traditional values and forms; whereas the other is of those who abandoned traditions and forms, due to the contact with the city" (BCSI, 1938, p. 190). Furthermore, he analysed the religiousness of the family, "school" and church, concluding that "the Orthodox

church, but not faith, in its everyday practice, does not satisfy the inner needs of the believers, and thus a decline of the institution is created, and a possibility for the animation of particular religious experiences"(BCSI, 1938, p. 199).
2. *Report on the folklore collected from Belinț* by prof. Tr. Topliceanu, who analysed folk poetry, erotic lyrics, traditions and customs at birth, marriage, death, magic incantations, superstitions and prejudices and found the power of tradition.
3. *Report on school* by prof. L. Anțila, who presented the history of the school in Belinț and described the school institutions in the commune, i.e. the kindergarten, the primary school and the secondary home industry school for girls, finding that "despite the efforts and endeavour of the teaching staff, in the given situation and with its present structure, it does not correspond, not even by far, to its purpose of training the youth as well as possible for the future occupation after they leave school" (BCSI, 1938, p. 267). Furthermore, the school building was improper, and the curriculum not practical enough, and the expert proposed the appointment of an agronomist in the school in view of organising a model farm.

The economic section approached aspects related to revenues, expenditure, price of industrial products, cultivated land, fruit trees, poultry, water supply etc., and elaborated three reports:

1. *Report on economic researches* by prof. eng. A. Lupan, who investigated 30 families, selecting 10 wealthy households, 10 average households and 10 very poor households and calculated the surface owned, the surface cultivated, the number of the members in the extended family, the income of the households, the family expenditure.
2. *Report on agricultural researches* by M. Demetrovici, who analysed the culture of plants, fruit trees, live stock breeding, household's endowment with farming tools and equipment.
3. *Report on hydrology and hydrotechnical works* by eng. V. Zbegan, who analysed the soil, the well water and the hydrographic situation of Belinț commune, situated between the courses of two rivers, Bega and Timiș, area subjected to the risk of flooding.

The legal section drew up two reports:

1. *Report on the agrarian reform* by Dr. I. Radu, who consulted the files from the rural court of Recaş and analysed the way the agrarian reform was realised, reform started in 1922, still unfinalised in 1934.
2. *Report on the legal manifestations in the family* by Dr. I. Radu, who researched: the legal patrimonial and personal manifestations (relatives, marriage, divorce, adultery, concubinage, legitimate and illegitimate births) and concluded that "from the results of the problems researched here it results that the following factors contribute to depopulation: the material situation and the system of endowment, frequent concubinages and adulteries, ignoring religious marriage and non-observance of its vows, early-age marriage, numerous divorces and the husband's life far form his family" (BCSI, 1938, p. 322)

The sociology and social policy section had the role of theoretical co-ordinator of the results obtained by the other sections, and also forwarded two reports:

1. *Report on the ethical-legal inquiry* by C. Grofşorean, who pointed out that the measures "required in order to fight against depopulation are medical-social in nature and the two groups are to be regulated by the state and its organisms" (BCSI, 1938, p. 352). The preventive measures are both medial-social in nature, are related to the youth education, as well as the social-political ones regulating marriage, spouses' age, fight against concubinage, fight against abortion, stimulation of birth rate by granting several facilities. The social-medical measures are imposed in the period of pregnancy and after birth for the reduction of infant death rate.
2. *Report on the ethical-legal researches* by A. Brudariu, who analysed the phenomenon of depopulation applying the ethical-legal question-naire underlying the realisation of the investigation in the Belinţ commune. Of the total 400 households they examined 60, "the household investigated are most representative, and the answers are typical and present the village image" (BCSI, 1938, p. 359). The questionnaire comprised 381 questions and studied several categories of problems: the system of property, the system of wealth production

and transmission within the family, personal and material relations among the family members; legal practices and customs.

On the 3rd of September 1934, at the closure of the works of the Royal Student's Team at Fibiş, His Majesty Carol the Second was presented a brief report on the situation found in the Belinţ village, as well as the solutions to be implemented. Thus, the report mentioned that "Banat's depopulation is due first of all to the very low birth rate, and second to the very high infant death rate.

The low birth rate is provoked first of all by a wilful restriction of birth rate – birth control – (...) voluntary procreations, which in a country with a more advanced civilisation replaced the archaic procreation.

Second, we may list the self-inflicted abortions, which are unusually numerous in Banat (...).

The causes of the excessive infant death rate are under the scrutiny of the medical-social section. Among the causes of this death rate we may anticipate first women's ignorance, their conservatism and in many cases their idleness, exhaustion and extreme fatigue.

The moral causes determining both contraception and abortion in Belinţ are: a) the weakening of the religious faith: children and young women go to church very rarely; absence of religious forms at civil marriages; b) exaggerated luxury: the overrating of luxury even among children.(...) c) sexual debacle , adultery, prostitution, just like in the city; d) large-scale concubinage; e) divorces (...); f) moral qualities like virginity and prudeness are despised; g) physical qualities like beauty, strength, health, diligence, are sacrificed for the wealth that is especially worshipped. All these are the causes for dissolution, disorganisation and failure of the Banat family.

Social causes: a) early sexual life, in concubinages and premature marriages, without religious forms, of 14-year old girls and 16-year old men; b) too frequent contacts with the city, from which they take all sorts of vices; c) propaganda against birth rate and the bad example of the Suabians with their so-called "zwei Kinder / two children" system, which often becomes "ein Kind / one child" and even "keine Kinder / no children" systems, because this allows them to live in comfort and cosiness and to consume the wealth inherited from their ancestors in a selfish manner; d) social diseases like TB, to a small extent, than alcoholism, venereal diseases, abortions. (...)

Economic causes: a) scarcity of subsistence means . (...) b) exhausting economic activity: the excessive labour of gardening, as they must sell their gardening produce themselves, hundreds of kms. away, two-way voyages, which also makes them be absent from home several months per year, disorganising family by the absence of men from the conjugal home. Poverty, uncertainty of sales markets, harsh working conditions, under-nourishment, budgetary deficit, these are several economic causes undermining the Banat family.

So as to conclude: the moral decay, social diseases and social customs, and excessive labour had weakened the strength of Belinț peasants, consuming their vital energy down to exhaustion. (...)

And thus: the depopulation of the Belinț commune is due to the lack of subsistence means progressive along the increase of the population and the living standards the population is used to. The lack of subsistence means is due to the lack of energy in order to achieve the possibilities of existence, and thus they prefer to wilfully restrain birth rate. The lack of energy is the effect of the organic weakening of the people, due to causes of moral, social and economic nature, listed above. In a word, the actual cause of depopulation is the firm will to not have children, will determined by a complex of dispositions: intellectual, moral., aesthetic, social and economic, specific for Banat"(BCSI, 1938, pp. 393 – 396).

The solutions proposed for the moral causes were: church choir, participation of children in church festivals accompanied by teachers, school uniforms, prizes, aids for the families with more than three children, obligativity of religious marriages, punishment of concubinage etc.

Solutions proposed for the social causes: interdiction of marriage under 18 years for girls and 20 for boys; attendance and graduation from the school of home industry, punishments for abortions, higher taxes for the childless families, free medical assistance, sanitary education in schools etc.

Solutions proposed for the economic causes: drainage of the flooded land, co-operatives for the produce sale, development of rural domestic industries etc.

The attentive investigation, by frames and manifestations, the deep analysis and the complexity of the researched phenomenon determined the exceeding of the two-week period initially decided, and thus, although the campaign was officially closed on the 2nd of September, the investigation of children (for the establishment of the demographic movement) continued until the 19th of September, and the male population was subjected to examination "in two Sundays in the months of September and October".

As regards the activity of the monographic team, C. Grofșorean mentioned that "from the ensemble of our investigation we may clearly conclude that the team was led by the same principles of collective observations governing also the monographs of the Romanian Social Institute of Bucharest. We shall set, based on these collective observations, through free and contradictory debates, in the united sections, our collective conclusions, as this is the only way we can give the Institute Committee the possibility to elaborated several collective proposals to subject to the entitled organisms, because the Banat-Crișana Social Institute does not aim exclusively at scientific purposes, but uses its scientific apparatus in view of finding rapid and unavoidable remedies, if we want to make sure the Romanian element does not lose its natural supremacy along the western frontier" (BCSI, 1938, p. 356).

Following the example of the RSI monographic teams, the BCSI got involved in the daily life of the Belinț inhabitants, carrying out, during the survey, a rich cultural activity, consisting in topics of general interest such as health, farming knowledge, medical assistance, medical examinations, prizes and subsidies granted to the meritous and poor farmers.

The closure festivity of the campaign was honoured by the presence of important personalities of scientific an public life: Professor D. Gusti, chairman of the RSI, Dr. Nistor, the county Prefect, Dr. Manuilă, the leader of the Fibiș royal team, The Chief Inspector of the County School Board, P. Râmneanțu.

After the end of the Belinț campaign, the official organisms were contacted (Prefect' Office, Mayor's Official sanitary institutions, Farming Chamber etc) regarding the situation in the locality, asking for the remedy of the situation.

D. Gusti appreciated the activity of the BCSI in the research of the depopulation phenomenon in a paper presented at the Romanian Academy as follows: "Depopulation of Banat proved, grace to the important works of the Timişoara Social Institute, to have a complex social causality: biologic, naturally, but determined by economic, religious, legal and moral factors" (Gusti, D., 1940, series III, vol. XXII).

2. The Sârbova campaign

The second campaign of the Institute took place in the *August 13th – September 3rd 1935*, at Sârbova, locality situated near the Belinţ commune (17 kms away) and near the city of Timişoara (27 kms away) and in this village the problem subjected to the study was focused on the same phenomenon, depopulation of the Banat village. In his foreword to the volume, C. Grofşorean motivated the objective of the research: "As we considered that one single research was not sufficient to penetrate all the secret nuances of the problems and in order to double-check our conclusions and the convictions acquired in the Belinţ investigation, the Committee had decided to continue the researches with the same objective, in the summer of 1935. Consequently the monographic team continued their works in the Sârbova commune, a similar all-Romanian village, situated in the region haunted by the plague of depopulation" (BCSI, 1939, p. 5).

The Sârbova campaign was preceded by the research performed by the statistic team, who used the RSI working instruments and completed the "family chart" and the "economic chart" and processed the data, and distributing them to the sections that elaborated the questionnaires necessary for the research.

This campaign, compared to the previous one, was attended by more persons, over 50 specialists in diverse fields and local intellectuals, and the teams were made according to the topics, ensuring thus the premises for the focusing of research on facts, phenomena and processes considered significant.

The medical-social team, made of the physicians Popovici V., Popovici M., Drăgan N., etc. examined the adult population from the perspective of dentistry, eyesight, STDs, TB and corporal hygiene. The sub-team made of Dr. Nemoianu and dr. Pruneş aided by two nurses examined children under 15 years of age from the medical and social viewpoint.

The legal team focused their attention on the investigation of the legal phenomena related to family. The team was made of Grofşorean C., Botiş E., Brudariu A., Ţenchea I., Porumb C., Ţigoianu C.

The economic team led by Dugăiaşu S., together with accountant Ciurceu M. and four assistants analysed the technical inventory of households, the tillable surface, the way of using the land, the farmers' labour technique.

The religious team made of the priests Şora M. and Şepeţan Gh. and the teacher Maxim I. studied the religious life of the villagers, morality, customs, as well as the exercise of the educational role by the family.

The education and folklore team, made of Sârbu V., Anţilă L., Bucătură M., reconstituted the history of the school and analysed the didactic means utilised, the school pupils nourishment, and the school situation and results.

The team led by Gh. Atanasiu limited its activity in this campaign, focusing its research on the house hygiene.

Furthermore, other teams conducted researches in Sârbova, i.e. the cosmological and anthropologic team led by Contrea A., as well as the household and domestic team led by Mrs. Adam-Munteanu.

This campaign applied the investigation or inquiry as general method, using the questionnaire as main instrument, associating the technique of the individual and collective interviews with direct observation and study of documents.

The Sârbova Report speaks about the manner of organising the BCSI field investigations. Thus, the minutes no.2 reads: "Dr. Radu, Secretary General of the Institute briefly presents the principle underlying the system of research adopted by the Institute. He shows the stages and the schedule of the sociologic monographs that the Institute shall conduct in the Sârbova commune (Timiş-Torontal county) in the period August 15th – September 2nd 1935" (BCSI, 1935, f. 5). Thus, in the first day of the campaign one realised the contact with the village inhabitants, they were explained the purpose of the research and the team members were introduced. The team visited the village and participated in the artistic show organised by the locals (as it was Sunday). The following day the research schedule was presented, along with the technique of organisation and deployment of researches and the results of the preliminary inquiry, as well as the teams allotment. There were daily reports on the evolution of activities, everything was mentioned in the minutes, the daily activity was written down by sections. The investigation method was applied, and the filled in questionnaires and charts were filed in the evening with the statistic office, by problems studied, and they could be consulted by all teams. The legal questionnaire (BCSI, 1935, f. 8) contained questions related to engagement, marriage, personal and material relations within the family, and the public law questionnaire was structured in two parts, the first focused on the persons' knowledge related to the constitutional law (BCSI, 1939, p. 271) more precisely: the organisation of the Romanian State, rights and obligations of citizens, whereas the second part was focused on administrative law, and the questioned entities were local authorities (BCSI, 1939, p. 261). Moreover, one applied another questionnaire treating the problem of concubinage (BCSI, 1939, p. 223), and M. Țigoianu elaborated the *Report on concubinage*. The leader of the legal team, dr. Grofșorean, elaborated the *Report on legal manifestations*, pointing out that "on the basis of the questionnaire one investigated the legal-family phenomena *in situ"* (BCSI, 1939, p. 223).

An intense activity was carried out by the medical-social section, who, in the three weeks, examined a number of 167 children of the total 174 aged under 15, as well as 482 adults of the total 624, "the inhabitants were distributed for examination – 40 persons per day – and the appointments were approximately set for certain hours" (BCSI, 1939, p. 75). Moreover, form the eye sight point of view, the doctors examined 650 persons. In order to have the general picture of the population's teeth they used the medical-dentistry questionnaire" (BCSI, 1935, vol. 62) and realised the dental record for 76% of the population, whereas the analysis of the inhabitants' corporal hygiene was made with the help of a questionnaire applied in 140 households (BCSI, 1939, p. 150). The members of the section elaborated the following reports:

– *Report on the medical and hygienic-social situation of the infantile population aged between 0 and 15* (I. Pruneș);
– *Report on the spreading of TB among the population over 15 years of age* (M. Popovici);

- *Report on the population's examination from the point of view of STDs and sexual life* (A. Maior);
- *Report on the population's examination regarding eye sight* (V. Popovici);
- *Report on the population's examination from the dentistry perspective* (N. Drăgan);
- *Report on the inhabitants' corporal hygiene* (Dimitrie Milota);
- *Report on the home hygiene* (Gh. Atanasiu).

In the *Report on the researches from the sanitary-veterinary perspective, live stock hygiene and zootechnical issued,* the veterinarian Radu Dimitrie drew the attention on the absence of veterinarians in the rural area, "a veterinarian doctor is forced to serve 25 to 30 communes" (BCSI, 1939, p. 217), as well as on the precarious knowledge peasants have in this field, for instance the "pest malady" that was discovered on the occasion of the research.

The domestic arts teacher Aurelia Adam-Munteanu, author of the *Report on researches in the field of population's nourishment,* analysed the population's feeding habits during seven weeks (after the end of the campaign), remarking three categories of families, giving details about "two very wealthy families, another with average material situation and another two families from among the poorest" (BCSI, 1939, p. 121).

The economic team realised the analysis, grouping the households in accordance with the land owned, and thus three categories of households resulted: pour households (owning 0 – 5 acres), average household (owning 5 – 20 acres) and rich households (owning over 20 acres). Of the total 172 existing households a number of 30 households were selected, 10 to illustrate each category, and they were considered representative: "a number of 10 characteristic households were studied, as the short delay did not allow their global investigation" (BCSI, 1939, p. 195). *The Report on the agricultural situation* was drawn up by S. Dugăiașu, delegate of the Ministry of Agriculture.

The report on the religious-moral life elaborated by Father Șora Melentie refers to the questionnaire used for the investigation of religious life. School (BCSI, 1939, p. 178) was analysed by M. Bucătură who elaborated the *Report on the people's school and culture.*

The historic report was completed on the basis of archive documents and through the interviews with the inhabitants conducted by Ilie Ghenadie. *The geographic report* as well as the human frame were analysed by Contea.

The activity of the legal team resulted in the *Report on the administrative organisation of the commune* elaborated by Emil Botiş and the *Report on the real estate situation, Real Estate Register and application of the agrarian reform* by A. Grozescu.

During the entire campaign a dispensary was established in the commune, providing medical examinations and treatment; an agrarian library was organised in the cultural home, conferences were held, the topics approached being of high interest for the local community: children rearing, hygiene of the pregnant woman, effects of alcoholism, fruit trees culture, land tilling; seeds and sowing; live stock diseases etc.; and the campaign was officially closed by a festivity.

Botiş E. drew up the "General report on the findings of facts and improvement solutions proposed by the Banat-Crişana Social Institute" comprising a synthesis of the depopulation causes: economic, moral, religious, biologic, medical, cultural, and the means considered appropriate for their elimination. The research conducted at Sârbova was not focused only on the depopulation phenomenon, but it also analysed the community from the sociologic viewpoint. The report tried to grasp "the totality the social phenomena found at Sârbova, with the necessary remedies" (BCSI, 1939, p. 11).

The volume "The Monograph of the Sârbova commune" co-ordinated by C. Grofşorean and E. Botiş, (392 p.) was published in 1939 and contained the aforementioned reports and the section "Musical contributions to the monograph of the Sârbova commune", section elaborated on a later date (in the year 1939) by the folklorist Ursu Nicolae at the request of the BCSI, in order to complete the Sârbova investigation with the musical part. The monograph of the Sârbova commune appeared in 2500 copies. Moreover, the photographic material of the campaign was presented in Bucharest at an exhibition organised by the Royal Foundations.

3. The Pojejena de Jos campaign

The third field trip of the BCSI monographers took place at *Pojejena de Jos*, locality situated on the shore of the Danube River, in the Boilers' Danube Shore, in the period *August 15th – September 3rd 1936*. This location was chosen as a result of a conference held by the General Inspector of the School Board S. Evuțian, who drew the attention on the denationalisation phenomenon of the Romanian element in that region under Romanian administration.

The research objectives were (Albert, C., 2002, p. 99):

a) "The establishment of our ethnic force in the Danube Shore area;
b) Establishment and repression of our existing maladies;
c) Observation and fight against sectarism".

The statistic team preceded the research following the model of the previous campaign, and thus, in the pre-investigation phase one elaborated the family charts and the economic charts, and the processed data were put at the disposal of the teams. The inquiry was conducted according to the method of Professor D. Gusti, analysing the local frames and manifestations using the methodological means applied in the previous campaigns. A number of 50 monographers participated in the research, permanent members and new members, intellectuals of the area, graduates of the sanitary and pedagogic school. The activity carried on by sections was the following (Negru, A., 1999, pp. 102 – 103):

– The cultural section was led by I. Miloia. The team researched the church and the religious manifestations, the religious folklore, the Serbianisation by religious modalities, the school, the cultural home, the archaeology and history the poetic patrimony.
– The economic section preserved the selection pattern of the 30 households (three categories), and the form was focused on the property, produce and expenditure; co-operation and fishmongery regime; labour, rest and personal hygiene.
– The social-political section analysed the system of property and its transfer, marriage, family relations.

- The legal section studied the regime of the former frontier properties – the problem of "occupations"; it applied the ethical-legal questionnaire;
- The medical-social section was divided by specialisations: children rearing and paediatrics; surgery and gynaecology; STDs; food and nourishment; house hygiene.
- The statistic section, led by I. Negru, conducted an analysis of birth and death rate of the population living on the Danube Shore.

In the report about the BCSI activity for the period April 1st 1935 – April 1st 1936 (BCSI, 1936, pp. 106 – 110) the cultural activity carried on by the Pojejena de Jos team was described. The BCSI members provided legal consulting and assistance as well as medical examinations and treatments, they held public-interest conference, organised cultural shows, helped establishing a library and distributed books and brochures.

From the results of the monographic investigation only a few articles were published (Bălan, C.C., 2001, pp. 239 – 240) in the Institute Journal, i.e.: *The monographic campaign at Pojejena de Jos* (C. Grofșorean, 1937); *The situation on the Danube Shore and the Romanian-Serbian litigation* (Iosef Jivan, 1940); *In the Danube Valley* (C. Grofșorean, 1941); *The religious and moral life in the Romanian Pojejena commune* (Melintie Șora, 1941); *Statistic of the Upper Danube Shore* (Negru, I., 1943); *Literary folklore of Pojejena de Jos* (Gh. Atanasiu, 1944).

4. The Ohaba Bistra campaign

The BCSI objective for the year 1937 as a priority of the agrarian section was the analysis of the situations of the Romanian colonists of Banat, project that was never materialised because of lack of funds, the subject being approached and presented in the BCSI Journal only through individual studies.

In 1938 the BCSI focused its attention on another problem, that of the transformation of the agrarian population into an industrial population, "the interesting process of the slow transformation of a population that until recently had agricultural activities" (BCSI, 1942, p. 144). This urbanisation phenomenon, characteristic for the Romania of that period, could be analysed at Ohaba Bistra, locality situated in the vicinity of the Ferdinand metallurgic works.

Consequently, the fourth monographic campaign took place at *Ohaba Bistra* in the period *August 3rd – September 4th 1938,* and the research was focused on the influence of the industrialisation process upon the Romanian autochthonous element "in order to investigate the issue of the industrialisation influence upon the Romanian autochthonous element, that is why we chose the Ohaba Bistra commune, as in the area between this commune and the Zăvoieni commune we see more concrete manifestations of the modern industry influence" (Nedelea, V., 1838, p. 130).

The pre-investigation realised by the statistic team started on the 18th of July (Grofşorean, C., 1938, f. 32), and the working instruments were analysed by specialists outside the Institute (BCSI, 1938, f. 10). The novelty of this campaign consisted in the common effort of the BCSI, the Royal Cultural Foundations "King Carol" and Astra, in view of getting acquainted with the realities of the Romanian village (BCSI, 1938, f. 29).

In accordance with the methodology of the Institute, preserving the structure and conception of the previous campaign, the following sections were established (Nedelea, V., 1938, pp. 130 – 138):

- The legal section, made of C. Grofşorean (team leader), E. Boriş, A. Brudariu, T. Stângu, M. Demetrovici and N. Gaşpar, who conducted investigations based on the previously elaborated questionnaires. Thus, on the basis of a 72-question questionnaire, a number of 23 families were interviewed regarding engagements, marriage, family relations. Further questionnaires were applied, i.e. ethical-legal (230 questions), political-social (124 questions) and the system of property (110 questions). Furthermore, the section studied cases of concubinage (4), divorce (2), mixed marriages (3) and incidents occurred in the factory (3) (Grofşorean, C., 1942, p. 144).
- The religious section, made of M. Şora and T. Stanca, studied 30 families and elaborated the family charts.
- The medical section, made of N. Gaşpar, I. Adam, I, Iovu, S. Bistrean, P. Sârbu elaborated 797 medical charts for adults and 247 medical-social charts for children, and also examined 236 children and adults from the neighbouring villages, whereas dr. Atanasiu researched the

homes. The dentistry sub-section examined 622 villagers (Grofşorean, C., 1942, p. 145).
- The economic section was numerous, made of 17 members, who interviewed 89% households on issues related to property, product, expenditure, generalities and labour questionnaires. "A total of 421 questions were asked regarding the household, grouped in 4 large chapters (…).Another 180 labour questionnaires were completed" (Nedelea V., 1838, p. 131).
- The zootechnical section, made of T. Matei and two students, analysed the livestock of the households of 77 families, finding the presence of pig pest and poultry cholera (BCSI, 1938, vol.33).
- The school section (Gh. Boran) researched primary education.
- The historic section studied the history of the commune, the history of the "Wealth Community, of the border guards regiment with the headquarters in Caransebeş with a local commander in Ohaba Bistra, as well as the history of the Ferdinand Works" (Grofşorean, C., 1942, pp. 145 – 146).
- The geographic section was made of I. Stiniguţă and T. Oancea.
- The section for the children's social hygiene led by Mrs. Mia Marian-Jaleş elaborated 191 charts for certifying the hygiene norms observance in the children rearing. They found a high death rate among infants aged between 0 and 1 year, proposing "the sending of at least two nurses who, through steady and skilled work, could remedy the present situation. What is really necessary is the establishment of a model dispensary (…) This dispensary could be founded with the help of the Ferdinand Works, where 90 % of the commune inhabitants work" (Marian-Jaleş, M., 1942, p. 127).
- The folklore section studied the musical tradition (N. Ursu, I Crişan), choreography (Iuliu Ilcă – Astra researcher), children's songs and games (A. Victor), church folklore (M, Şora), literary folklore (M. Marian-Jaleş, Gh. Atanasiu) (Grofşorean, 1942, p. 146).
- The section for labour, corporal hygiene, rest and household led by A. Percea and sixty investigators analysed 30 families and performed guidance actions.
- The ethnographic section was led by E. Secoşan.

According to the already established tradition, each evening the team members used to talk about the material collected "(…) discussions take place in the officers' mess location, and the team members communicate to the team leader, dr. C. Grofşorean, all the observations of the day" (BCSI, 1938, no. 484).

The cultural actions consisted in conferences on different topics of interest (children's diseases, alcoholism, nourishment), the ethnographic exhibition realised by Elena Secoşan, the triptych executed by P. Oancea, the installation of a fruit drier, the distribution of farming brochures. (Grofşorean, C., 1942, p. 146).

The studies resulted from the Ohaba-Bistra campaign were published in the BCSI Journal. Among them we may list:

- C. Grofşoreanu in the paper *At Ardeal Iron Gates* affirmed that "based on the data collected from the interviewed persons, we find in the case of many families a certain wellbeing, well developed economic spirit and a genuine desire of progress, i.e. of urbanisation" (Grofşorean, C., 1942, p. 639);
- The economic issues debated by Paul Cocârlan in his paper *Introduction to the economic-social study of the Ohaba Bistra village* referred to the effect of industrialisation (Cocârlan, P., 1941, pp. 215 – 277);
- In his paper *Urbanisation of the Romanian peasant,* Emil Botiş (Botiş, E., 1940, pp. 639 – 652) analysed the manifest and latent effects of the urbanisation phenomenon;
- *From the past of the Ohaba Bistra commune* by Gh. Cotoşman (Cotoşman, Gh., 1942, pp. 620 – 629);
- *Children rearing at Ohaba Bistra* by Adam Ionel (Adam, I., 1942, pp. 101 – 107);
- *Legal report on the Ohaba Bistra commune* by Tr. Stângu (Stângu, Tr., 1942, pp. 236 – 249)
- *Children's social hygiene in Ohaba Bistra* by Mia Marian-Jaleş (Marian-Jaleş, M., 1942, pp. 127 – 129);
- *Religious and moral life in the Ohaba Bistra commune* by Melintie Şora (Şora, M., 1943, pp. 419 – 442);
- *Monographic report on the public primary school of the Ohaba Bistra commune* by Gh. Boran (Boran, Gh., 1939, pp. 21 – 42);

- *Musical folklore from the Ohaba Bistra commune* by Nicolae Ursu (Ursu, N., 1938, pp. 111 – 115);
- *Choreographic report on Ohaba Bistra* by Ilca Iuliu (Ilca I., 1942, pp. 122 – 126).

In the vision of the BCSI, this campaign had to be a first step in the research of the effects of organisation, and they were planning ample studies in Reşiţa (influence of metallurgic industry) and Anina, with extension to the Jiu Valley.

In order to complete the Ohaba-Bistra researches a visit to Reşiţa was organised in order to examine the Stavila district. "For this purpose we organised the visit of two teams, one monographic made of around 5 permanent team members (…) and the second team was made of 15 volunteers (graduates) precisely at Reşiţa, in order to examine in the workers' district Stavila the situation of the already urbanised Romanian workers, and in Reşiţa-Română the situation of Romanian farmers, who have a direct and constant contact with the factories, without abandoning their farming activities. It was an extraordinarily interesting moment. In Ohaba-Bistra the process is reversed. Only a number of 20 families still preserve the farming activity" (Albert, C., 2002, p. 113). Unfortunately this ample project remained only in the draft phase, and the intention to continue the research in 1939 was not accepted by Dimitrie Gusti.

5. The Almăj Valley campaign

The loss of autonomy, along with the coming into force of the Law of Social Service (October 18th 1938), turned the BCSI into a branch of the Romania's Institute of Social Researches and functioned under the name of Romania's Institute of Social Researches. Timişoara Regional Branch. In these conditions, the Institute was funded by the Romania's Institute of Social Researches, working "within the frame and under its scientific guidance" (BCSI, 1939).

This integration led to the modification of certain articles from the BCSI Statute, i.e. the provision stipulating the creation of a permanent monographic team remunerated from the regional branch budget.

The members appointed (acc. to art. 27) by the Romania's Institute of Social Researches were the experienced monographers C. Grofşorean, E. Botiş, Gh. Atanasiu, A. Grozescu, M. Bucătură, M. Şora, E. Secoşan, I. Stiniguţă, P. Cocârlan, C. Teodorescu, G. Birăescu, N. Ursu, N. Drăgan, A. Percea, I, Crişan, C. Coloşan (Herseni, T., 1939, no. 28208).

From this subordinated position the Banat Institute no longer succeeded in continuing the investigations from the prior year related to the influence of industrialisation on the Romanian peasant in the Reşiţa area.

A new stage followed, that of investigating, instead of individual villages, entire districts, idea contested by C. Grofşorean: "Since when is the district a social unit? We knew that is was a very variable administrative unit and we also know that the social unit is the family, the village, the problem region, but a district?" (Grofşorean, C., 1939, no. 132/487/5) arguing that the small number of members cannot monograph a district, which means the investigation of all villages, if we want to elaborate a serious work.

The decision of Romania's Institute of Social Researchers was made, and the objective set was the Bozovici District , more precisely the elaboration of the monograph of the model district Bozovici, situated in the Caraş county, which comprised 16 villages and 3 colonies, the topic being the grasping of the urbanisation of the Banat village "as product of the peasant autochthonous civilisation", thus "a synthesised monograph of the Banat border" meant to discover the problems of the area.

Professor Dimitrie Gusti hoped to conduct the monographs of all the villages in the country, but this would have required very much time. Some of his disciples (among whom Anton Golopenţia) suggested other ways: "the condition was however that the monograph, from integral, bearing on the entire "social unit of the village", and going to the exhaustion of the subjects, remains limited to several more modest but essential "problems", and more precisely circumscribed" (Stahl, H.H., 1971, p. 90).

Consequently, the problems considered essential in the "pilot village" (Nerej, Vrancea county; Drăguş for the study of the Olt Country; Runcu for the study of the northern area of the Gorj county) were researched in the villages from the respective geographic area. The same idea, but presented in another form, leads to the so-called "model districts" starting from the same idea to research an extended territorial space, but also with the purpose to elaborate a documentation in view of an action of regional systematisation: "by studying the complex of local situation, one could elaborate a plan of local actions, started simultaneously along several lines, mobilising the entire group of technicians of all specialisations" (Stahl, H.H., 1971, p. 92).

The campaign conducted in the Bozovici district started on the 29th of June 1939, where only four village of the total 16 were investigated: Bozovici, Bănia, Moceriş and Borlovenii Noi.

The indirect investigation was realised by the self-administration of the questionnaire, which was distributed to the district Praetor on July 1st 1939. The "administrative" questionnaire, made of 51 questions related to the activity of the local administration, contained: "the history of the commune administration, its patrimony, the functioning of the administrative services, fulfilment of the procedures, decisions of the Mayor's Office, houses numbering, incorporations in the public domain, communal taxes, monitoring of public revenues, expropriations for public utility, election lists, public works executed, operation of the public service for petitions, complaints, optimisation proposals etc." (Albert, C., 2003, p. 13).

The path of the questionnaire was the following: the praetors had to distribute the questionnaires to the mayor's offices of the 16 localities, they had to be filled in with the help of notaries, and the answers had to be collected in Timişoara. This sequence can be followed from the correspondence of the Timişoara Regional Branch with the Praetor's Office of the Bozovici district (Albert, C., 2003, p. 115):

Social Service
Romania's Institute of Social Researches
Timişoara Regional Branch
The monographic team of the Bozovici district (Caraş)
July 1st 1939
Addressed to the Praetor's Office of the Bozovici district
Mr. Praetor,

In accordance with the orders of the Prefect's Office of the Caraş county no. 9865 and 9893 of June 27th 1939 we have the honour to ask you to request all the Mayor's offices of the communes of this district to send, until the 15th of July 1939, the following data:

1) The filling in of the enclosed questionnaire (the administrative questionnaire)
2) The situation of the cashing ins and the residual taxes (direct, additional and communal) on the 1st of June 1939.

The situation of the cashing ins from the debts of the communal ephories from the past residues and the debts of the current year drawn up on the 1st of June 1939.

4) The table of births in the commune during the entire year 1938, male and female babies born alive; male and female still borns; deaths; remaining population.
5) A copy of the questionnaire ordered as no. Praetor's Office Bozovici 349 of February 17th 1939 and the Prefect's Office Caraş no. 2436 of February 14th 1939.
6) A copy of the communes' 1939/40 budget revision.

The above data filled in will be collected and send to the Institute of Social Researches of Romania, Timişoara Regional Branch, Polytechnic School of Timişoara.

Moreover, please request the district notaries that they are liable for the accuracy of the data, that will be checked. The data after processing will be published in the monograph of the Bozovici district by the Institute of Social Researches of Romania, whose acting president is His Majesty King Carol the Second.

General Secretary	Director of the Team
Team Head	Dr. C. Grofşorean
Dr. E. Botiş	

The documents received from the Praetor's Office of the Bozovici district were included in the Annual Report on the general state of the Bozovici district, for the year 1938 containing 13 sections (Albert, C., 2003, pp. 35 – 55):

I. *The geographic and administrative situation.* The Bozovici district, one of the six divisions of the Caraş county, has 16 communes with six circuit notary offices in Bozovici, Bănia, Dalboşeţ, Prigor, Prilipeţi, Rudăria. The composing communes are compact settlements, except the Şopotul Nou commune, which is organised in a system of temporary dwellings. The hilly terrain is good for farming, the land strip of a family ranges between 2 and 6 acres, and the woods, covering a large part of the district, is the property of the Caransebeş Wealth Community, the communes being co-owners.

II. *Population.* The number of the population of the 16 communes at the end of 1938 was of 24299 inhabitants, decreasing from the 1930 census, phenomenon that was manifest in the entire Banat.

III. *The population's movement.* In the district, for the year 1939, the following were recorded: 477 births, 171 marriages, 26 divorces and 586 deaths, and the natural growth was negative. The causes of the low birth rate are the progressive poverty of the population, the lack of hygiene rules, the high number of abortions, the marriages between very young people, the model of a single-child family, alcoholism, syphilis.

IV. *The cultural, moral and religious state of the population.* In the district, the number of the pupils enrolled in primary school is of 2290, and attendance ranges between 65 and 93%. Of the 17 churches existing in the Bozovici district, 15 are Orthodox and 2 are Roman-Catholic, as most inhabitants are of Orthodox faith, except those of the Ravensca commune and a small number of Bozovici inhabitants who are Roman-Catholic. The two Cultural Homes of Rudăria and Prigor were established by the Royal Teams. In Lăpuşnicul Mare a Cultural Home was built, with the support of Mr. E. Gherman, which has a show hall, dispensary, library and baths for the villagers, and in Bozovici a National Home was functioning, disposing of a show hall (used also as mute cinema) and a library.

V. *The state of the public opinion in the communes.* "The new Constitution was voted in unanimity by the district inhabitants".

VI. *The population's economic status.* The inhabitants provide for their decent living by cultivating the land and breeding live stock.

VII. *The sanitary condition* had improved grace to the presence, in 1938, of a team of physicians sent by the Ministry of Health who, beside curative medicine, were preoccupied by the rural hygiene.
VIII. *The sanitary veterinary situation.* The sanitary service performed diverse preventive vaccinations.
IX. *The economic status of the political communes.* The revenues of the communes are low, they do not own domains that could produce incomes, that is why they do not have the capacity to cover the general needs.
X. *The zootechnical condition of communes.* The absence of pastures caused the decrease the number of live stock. Due to the milk acquisitions of the cheese factories of Bozovici and of the milk producers of Prilipeți and Bănia the inhabitants of the area started to increase the number of their animals.
XI. *The financial situation of the communes.* The communes have difficulties in covering the expenditure, and in the population, for the financial year 1938 – 1939 one remarked a higher payment capacity compared to the previous years.
XII. *The accomplishments of 1938* were: ways and roads; cleaning of communal ponds; construction of communal stables, bridges, aids for the renovation of churches, schools etc.
XIII. *Plans for the future.* Due to the low budget, communes do not have the capacity to execute important works such as "constructions, communal baths, Cultural Homes", and they are limited to urgent works.

Thus, the Mayor's Office complied with the request of the Caraș county prefect's office, and filled in the forms, offering a rich material about the 16 communes composing the Bozovici district.

The monographic team who participated in the Bozovici district campaign was divided into the statistic team, made of prof. Ilie Stâniguță, Titus Oancea, Ion Maxim and Mircea Olariu, who filled in the family charts, and the proper team, made of 13 members: Dr. C. Grofșorean, Dr. Emil Botiș, Dr. Elena Secoșan, Dr. Alexandru Grozescu, Marius Bucătură, Dr. Nicolae Ursu, Gheorghe Atanasiu, Paul Cocârlan, prof. Romeo Feraru, Aurora Baicu, Traian Stângu Gheorghe Ionescu and

V. Nedela who then analysed in detail the frames and manifestations of the place studied previously by the statistic team.

The team were assisted by the notaries and teachers of the researched villages, as well we by twenty graduates, in accordance with the Law of the Social Service (Herseni, T., 1939).

Although it was not possible to elaborate a monograph, the studies realised in the Bozovici district campaign were published in the BCSI Journal:

- The cosmic frame was studied by prof. Stiniguță, and the papers he published were entitled *The Almăj Valley* with the geographic description, forms and limits of the Almăj Valley, mining ores in the depression (Stiniguță, I., 1940a, pp. 25 – 32; Stiniguță, I., 1940b, pp. 134 – 142).
- *The historic chronicle of the Almăj* by Coriolan Burlacu (Burlacu, C., 1941, pp. 33 – 46; Burlacu, C., 1942a, pp. 58 – 78; Burlacu, C., 1942b, pp. 225 – 235), who participated in the investigation within the Social Service, but had performed researches since 1912 in Mehadia, starting from the information from old church books, and in the period 1935 – 1938 continued the investigations acting in the teams of the Royal Cultural Foundation in the Rudăria commune.
- *The Dacians' country* (Grofșorean, C., 1940, pp. 1 – 12) describes the institution of the family community conferred on the basis of the Banat family wellbeing and *A Dacian-Wallachian eagles' nest* (Grofșorean, C., 1943, pp. 221 – 279) where C. Grofșorean presents fragments from charts with the affirmations of the subjects from the Almăj Valley campaign.
- *Four Almăj communes. Monographic researches at Borlovenii Noi, Bozovici, Moceriș and Bănia* by Traian Birăescu (Birăescu, T., 1942, pp. 563 – 594), the study presents: structure of the population, dynamics of the population, ethic and religious structure, dwelling, health condition of the inhabitants etc.
- *School and education of the Almăj population* by Marius Bucătură (Bucătură, M., 1940, pp. 344 – 351) presents the history and content of education and national schools.
- *The hygiene of the Almăj home* by Gh. Atanasiu (Atanasiu, Gh., 1940a, pp. 163 – 169; Atanasiu, Gh., 1940b, pp. 263 – 267) presents

the conclusions related to the aspects of households and the home hygiene.
- *A wedding in the Almăj Valley* by Nicolae Ursu (Ursu, N., 1940, pp. 469 – 494) describing the songs and dances practised at the wedding.
- *Almăj sources* by Elena Secoșan (Secoșan, E., 1940a, pp. 115 – 133; Secoșan, E., 1940b, pp. 339 – 343) presents the home industry from Almăj, weavings, costumes, arrangement of the home interior, and the study is completed by black and white, and colour images.

This monographic campaign conducted in the Almăj Valley was the last vast research of the BCSI.

6. The Naidăș campaign

In the summer of 1942 (August 15th – 30th), despite all the difficulties of that period, BCSI decided the resuming of the field researches at Naidăș, accepting also the support of Ilie Marcu who was willing "to subsidise the expenditure of a monographic team of BCSI to work this summer in his native village, the commune of Naidăș in Caraș" (Cosma, A., 1942, MD 34/9745).

The commune of Naidăș, situated in the vicinity of the Yugoslavian border between Biserica Albă and Sasca Montană, was an isolated commune, with almost unexisting infrastructure, no connection to the railroad, only communal roads unpracticable in certain period, as C. Grofșorean stated in the Research Report of 1942, "it was a locality entirely isolated from the rest of the world and the country" (Bălan, C.C., 2004, p. 86).

The objectives of the study were: the phenomenon of denationalisation due to the Serbian influence, a phenomenon analysed in 1936 at Pojejena too; depopulation, that constituted the object of the first two campaigns at Belinț and Sârbova, as well as the richness of the folklore analysed in all the monographic campaigns. "Naidăș presents a special interest because this village hides old Romanian traditions and a folklore of incomparable value. Old people of Naidăș still tell the wonderful legends, sing the remarkable ballads, songs and ancestral music, and the people's customs and superstitions have found a secular cradle here" (Cosma, A., 1942, MD 34/9745).

The monographic team was small, being made of eight persons: C. Grofşorean (legal issues), E. Secoşan (textile folklore), N. Ursu (musical folklore), Gh. Atanasiu (literary folklore), V. Ardelean (linguistic folklore), O. Borza (study of the region's flora), Gh. Ciorman (economic situation), Gh. Ionescu (plan of the area).

The statistic team, co-ordinated by Tr. Birăescu, conducted the preliminary statistic investigation, applying a census chart comprising data about the persons in the households, homes, home hygiene, farming land, occupations etc. The results obtained are presented in the work *The commune of Naidăş in the light of figures,* where Tr. Birăescu (Albert, C., 2003, pp. 363 – 375) presents the structure of the commune from the social and economic perspective. Of the 551 households, 82 did not answer the questionnaire, as in 27 the "head of the home" refused to respond, while in the remaining 55 the following situations were encountered: some were abandoned / not inhabited (37) or the head of the family was not available. The 469 households were inhabited by 1972 persons, the houses, in a percentage of 74.5%, were made of wood, and the two-room model was predominant (48.7%). According to religion, most of the population is Orthodox, and according to nationally "the commune of Naidăş is the type of the purely Romanian commune, with over 98% Romanians, 3 Hungarian inhabitants, 1 Czech inhabitant and 35 Gypsies, all settled in the commune, with their own houses" (Albert, C., 2003, p. 365). The paper also comprises data about the civil status "305 children / aged between 0 and 14 / legitimate, 37 illegitimate children, 105 singles, 1048 married, 314 widows or widowers, 18 divorced persons and 148 persons in de facto relationships" (Albert, C., 2003, p. 367); schooling level "more than half of the women cannot read or write and one in four men is illiterate, the most numerous population with complete primary education is encountered among the groups between 14 and 34 years of age" (Albert, C., 2003, p. 368); the distribution of the farming property; cultures (vineyards); craftsmen of the commune, occupations of the inhabitants; numerical evolution of the population. An alarming issue was discovered from the demographic point of view, i.e. "there were only 4 infants born alive to 1000 inhabitants, in the years 1941 – 1942" (Albert, C., 2003, p. 365). The obvious demographic decline was not due to changes in the behaviour, but to the maintenance of the "typically Banat behaviour" encountered also at Belinț and Sârbova. This phenomenon was highlighted also in the work of Mrs. Cornelia C. Bălan *Applied sociology*, where in Chapter IV she presents *The monograph of the Naidăș commune. Sociologic analysis of the peoples culture,* where she affirms that "after 1942, the depopulation phenomenon has gradually grown. On the 1st of January 1996, the population of the village was of 988 persons, which represents one third of the population living there in 1900, half of the population of 1942 and 15% less than the population of 1982" (Bălan, CC., 2004, p. 94). As for the demographic indices, the author points out "In each year when monographic researches were conducted (1942, 1982 and 1996), almost invariably there were at least two deaths corresponding to one single birth" (Bălan, CC., 2004, p. 97).

In another paper, *The health of the Naidăș commune*, Tr. Birăescu forwarded a report on the basis of the medical charts elaborated by the circuit doctor for more than 150 children aged between one and 15 years of age, finding normal births, on term, healthy children, pointing out that "the results of this examination gives us a pretty clear image about the health of tomorrow's Naidăș" (Albert, C., 2003, p. 391 – 393). Furthermore, he stated that one should find the modalities meant to eliminate / improve the system of 1 child-2 children existing in the Banat families.

The work *Ethical-legal report* by C. Grofșorean presents in its first part the system of the property, and in the second part the ethical-legal findings resulted from the application of the questionnaire – structured in four sections: 1. Marriage: engagement, marriage conclusion, personal relations among the family members, material relations within the family; 2. Obligations; 3. Legislature and customs; 4. Influence of the city (Albert, C., 2003, pp. 396 – 406) –, and the last part presents a comparison with the neighbouring villages.

Atanasiu Gh. selected a rich material, consisting in 13 ballads, 31 poems, 31 rhymed shouts, 23 songs, 19 stories, and due to the fact that certain ballads and poems have their own melody, it was caught by N. Ursu, whereas E. Secoșan describes in the paper *Folk costume of Naidăș* the beauty of the traditional costumes, of the woven materials made of hemp, wool, cotton, as well as the arrangement of the Naidăș homes (BCSI, 1942).

The monograph of the Naidăş commune was scheduled for publication in 1944, the manuscript handed over to the printing house had around 400 pages, and a number of 1000 copies were to be printed (Albert, C., 2002, p. 127). The volume elaborated by Naidăş monographic team had never been published, only the results of the investigations were partially recovered.

The correspondence between C. Grofşorean and Professor D. Gusti certifies the existence of the manuscript as well as the support for the printing of the volume (Gusti, D., 1943). From other two letters sent to Professor D. Gusti the title variants were identified :"1. Monograph of the Naidăş commune (Caraş county), sociologic analysis regarding literature, costumes and customs; 2. Sociologic analysis of the Naidăş commune (Caraş county) regarding literature, music, costumes and customs" (Grofşorean, C., 1944, D.J.C.S.A.N), as well as the structure of the chapters in the volume: " the content would be the following: 1. Your Excellency's foreword, very brief, to thank the Ministry for covering the printing costs; however, if you cared to express this homage on behalf of the Central Institute, then (…) we shall also need a foreword written by myself, then my general report, according to the prior usances. 4. Report to (…) by Mr. Tr. Birăescu. 5. Report of Mr. Atanasiu regarding literary folklore. 6. Report of M.Ursu about the musical folklore. 7. The ethnographic report by Mrs. Secoşan, 8. The ethno-botanical report by Mr. Borza, and 10. My ethical-legal report. After the studies there will be three black and white photos and 8 coloured photographs" (Albert, C., 2003, p. 361).

The Naidăş campaign concluded the series of the monographic campaigns, nevertheless the BCSI continued the series of public conference and forged plans for the future, expressing their desire to elaborate the history of Banat "at the same time we wish to elaborate a history of Banat, integrating the past of this region into the general history of the nation" (Albert, C., 2002, p. 127)

Conclusions

Remarkable personality of his epoch, world-famous scientist, man of culture, Dimitrie Gusti gained an outstanding recognition as sociologist both in the country and abroad. This prestigious place he earned was due both to his doctrine, interesting and rich in ideas, and to his capacity of initiation, organisation and co-ordination of the investigations of social reality in our country, with the enthusiastic support of an active team of collaborators.

Founder of a sociologic system, Dimitrie Gusti is original by the way he conceived social reality and sociology as science. Like other fellow sociologists, he had grasped the fact that sociology could no longer ignore reality.

In the period between the two World Wars, the "Monographic School", created and guided by Professor D. Gusti, set the cornerstones of the Romanian modern sociology with an important international echo in the sociology of the time. It is characterised by the systematic organisation of campaigns for the direct investigation of social reality with "complex interdisciplinary teams", initially organised within the Sociology Seminar of the Sociology Chair within the University of Bucharest, and then expanded throughout the country grace to a network of dedicated institutes.

The rural studies were the central axis of the Bucharest Sociologic School. The originality of the Gusti School paradigm consists in the fact that "it is the first School of Sociology that created a methodology of comparative-progressive research of social units, from family and village as social units to the super-rural communities and from the latter to the national societies and to the international units created, made of groups of nations such as the League of Nations or those attested by Paul H. Stahl's Balkan ethno-sociology , from which one can leap to the science of the social unit called humanity" (Bădescu, I., 2005, p. 7).

We should reveal the effort of the Bucharest Sociologic School in its active involvement in the life and labour of people for its knowledge and the attempt to answer the questions raised by social reality. The Bucharest Sociologic School carried out its entire activity under the motto: "social science and reform" as well as "knowledge and action in the service of the nation".

The establishment of the BCSI took place in 1932, after the creation of the RSI, following its example both as regards structure and set goals, and as regards the research activities conducted. An essential role in the establishment and the activity of the institute was played by the remarkable intellectuals of the region who had attended serious studies in Budapest (as for instance Dr. Cornel Grofşorean) or in the country's academic centres. We should remark the involvement in the activities of social reality research of personalities with important status and social role in the region, who supported or attracted personalities and institutions from the area, either with the purpose of concrete involvement in the researches conducted (priests, teachers, doctors), or in the financing of the activities;

Unlike the monographs conducted by the Bucharest Sociologic School, the monographs conducted by Banat-Crişana Social Institute were usually focused on one social issue, appreciated as being of stringent importance in the area (depopulation of Banat areas is a common theme, along with other specific topics: influence of the industrialisation process on the farming population, the phenomenon of denationalisation of the Romanian element, the richness of the folklore). However, we may find the fact that, in the intention of identifying the deep causes of the phenomena studied, the monographic teams used the methods and perspective utilised by the monographers of the Bucharest school (monograph, problem charts, questionnaire-based investigation, interviews, analysis of social documents).

Bibliography

Adam, I. (1942). "Puericultura la Ohaba Bistra / Children Rearing at Ohaba Bistra". In J. B.C.S.I., year X (Jan. – Feb. 1942), pp. 101 – 107.

Albert, C. (2002). *Cercetare monografică în Banat / Monographic research in Banat. (1859 – 1948)*. Timişoara: Editura / Editions Modus P.H.

Albert, C. (2003). *Documentele Institutului Social Banat-Crişana / Documents of the Banat-Crişana Social Institute*. Timişoara: Editura / Editions Mirton.

Amzăr, D.C. (1929). "Drăguşul. Aşezarea şi munca satului / Drăguş. Village location and labour". in *Poşta informativă / Informative Bulletin*, year II, (Oct. 1929), no. 40 – 41, pp. 21 – 22.

Atanasiu, Gh. (1940a). "Igiena casei în Almăj / Hygiene of the Almăj home". In J.B.C.S.I., year VIII (Feb. – March 1940), no. 28 – 29, pp. 163 – 169.

Atanasiu, Gh. (1940b). "Igiena casei în Almăj / Hygiene of the Almăj home". In J.B.C.S.I., year VIII (Apr. 1940), nr. 30, pp. 263 – 267.

Atanasiu, G. (1944). "Folclor literar din Pojejena de Jos / Literary folklore in Pojejena de Jos". In J. B.C.S.I., year XII (Jan. – Apr. 1944), pp. 100 – 114.

Atanasiu, G. (1944). "Folclor literar din Pojejena de Jos / Literary folklore in Pojejena de Jos". In J. B.C.S.I., year XII (Sept. – Dec. 1944), pp. 277 – 292.

Banat-Crişana Social Institute (BCSI). (1938). *Anchetă monografică în comuna Belinţ / Monographic survey in the Belinţ commune*, "Tipografia Românească", Timişoara.

Banat-Crişana Social Institute (BCSI). (1939). *Monografia comunei Sârbova / Monograph of Sârbova commune*, Timişoara.

Batâr, D. (2003). *Sociologie. Probleme teoretice şi analize ale investigaţiilor de teren / Sociology. Theoretical problems and analyses of field investigations.* ediţia a III-a revizuită / 3rd ed. rev., Sibiu: Editura / Editions Psihomedia.

Bădescu, I. (1981). *Satul contemporan şi evoluţia lui istorică / The contemporary village and its historical evolution.* Bucureşti: Editura Ştiinţifică şi Enciclopedică / Bucharest: Scientific and Encyclopaedic Editions.

Bădescu, I. (2005). "Şcoala Gusti: perenitatea unei paradigme / The Gustian School: perennity of a paradigm". In Revista / Journal *Sociologie Românească / Romanian Sociology,* vol III, no. 2, p. 7.

Bădescu, I., Cucu-Oancea, O. (coord.). (2005). *Dicţionar de sociologie rurală/ Dictionary of rural sociology.* Bucureşti / Bucharest: Editura / Editions Mica Valahie.

Bădescu, I., Dungaciu, D., Baltasiu, R. (1996). *Istoria sociologiei – teorii contemporane / History of sociology – contemporary theories,* vol. 1, Bucureşti / Bucharest: Editura / Editions Eminescu.

Bădina, O. (1965). *Dimitrie Gusti. Contribuţii la cunoaşterea operei şi activităţii sale / Dimitrie Gusti. Contributions to the knowledge of his work and activity.* Bucureşti / Bucharest: Editura Ştiinţifică / Scientific Editions.

Bădina, O. (1966). *Cercetarea sociologică concretă. Tradiţii româneşti / Concrete sociologic research. Romanian traditions.* Bucureşti / Bucharest: Editura Politică / Political Editions.

Bădina, O., Neamţu, O. (1967). *Dimitrie Gusti. Viaţă şi personalitate / Dimitrie Gusti. Life and personality.* Bucureşti / Bucharest: Editura Tineretului / Youth Editions.

Bălan, C.C. (2001). *Institutul Social Banat Crişana (1932 – 1946). Recuperarea culturală şi sociologică a moştenirii Institutului Social Banat Crişana / The Banat-Crişana Social Institute (1932 – 1946). Cultural and sociologic recovery of the heritage of the Banat- Crişana Social Institute* Timişoara: Editura / Editions Augusta.

Bălan, C.C. (2004). *Sociologie aplicată. Monografia centrată pe problemă / Applied sociology. The problem-focused monograph.* Bucureşti / Bucharest: Editura / Editions Tritonic.

BCSI (1933), "Statutele Institutului Social Banat-Crişana / Statutes of the Banat-Crişana Social Institute". In *J.B.C.S.I.,* year I (1933), no. 1, p. 35.

BCSI (1933). "Dare de seamă asupra activității de la 24 iunie 1932 până la 1 iulie 1933 / Report of activity between June 24th 1932 and July 1st 1933". In *J.B.C.S.I.*, year I (1933), no. 2 – 5, pp. 81 – 83.

BCSI (1934). "Raportul Secretariatului general despre activitatea I.S.B.C. de la 30 ianuarie 1933 la 31 martie 1934 / Report of the Secretary General about the BCSI activity between January 30th 1933 and March 31st 1934". In *J.B.C.S.I.*, year II (1934), no. 6 – 9, pp. 85 – 90.

BCSI (1934). "Raportul annual / Annual Report". In *J.B.C.S.I.*, year II (1934), no. 5, Official part.

BCSI (1934). *Raport annual / Annual Report*. In T.C.L., Fund "BCSI.", mss. V, vol. 94, 31 March 1934.

BCSI (1934). *Adresă I.S.B.C. – Prefectura Timiş-Torontal / Notification of BCSI to the Prefect's Office of Timiş-Torontal*. In T.C.L., Fund "BCSI.", mss. V, vol. 94, no. 153/1934.

BCSI (1934). *Adresă I.S.B.C. – Prefectura Timiş-Torontal / Notification of BCSI to the Prefect's Office of Timiş-Torontal*. In T.C.L., Fund "BCSI.", mss. V, vol. 94, no. 162/1934.

BCSI (1935). T.C.L., D IV 4867, no. 117/1935.

BCSI (1935). *Condica proceselor verbale / Register of minutes* In T.C.L., Fund "BCSI.", mss. V, vol. 45, June 19th – July 5th 1935, s. 5.

BCSI (1935). *Condica proceselor verbale / Register of minutes* In T.C.L., Fund "BCSI.", mss. V, vol. 45, June 19th – July 5th 1935, s. 8.

BCSI (1935). *Chestionar medico-stomatologic, Sârbova / Medical-dentistry questionnaire, Sârbova*. In T.C.L., Fund "BCSI.", mss. V, vol. 62.

BCSI (1936). "Raport asupra activității I.S.B.C. din Timişoara pe intervalul de timp de la 1 aprilie 1935 – 1 aprilie 1936 / Report of activity of BCSI Timişoara for the period April 1st 1935 – April 1st 1936". In *J.B.C.S.I.*, year IV (1936), no. 16, pp. 106 – 110.

BCSI (1938). "Echipa monografică a Institutului Social Banat-Crişana lucrează intens pentru ridicarea elementului românesc / The BCSI monographic team is working hard for the awakening of the Romanian element". In *Vocea Banatului / Voice of Banat*, year IX, no. 484.

BCSI (1938). T.C.L., Fund "BCSI.", mss. V, vol. 162, s. 10.

BCSI (1938). *Scrisoare I.S.B.C. – N. Buteanu / Letter from BCSI to N. Buteanu* In T.C.L., Fund "BCSI.", mss. V, vol. 43, 6 Aug. 1938, s. 29.

BCSI (1938). *Proces-verbal / Minutes*. In T.C.L., Fund "BCSI.", mss. V, vol. 33, 14 Aug. 1938.
BCSI (1939). *Proiect de statute cu privire la colaborarea dintre I.S.B.C. și Institutul de Cercetări Sociale a României / Draft of the statutes regarding the co-operation between BCSI and Romania's Institute of Social Researches* In T.C.L., Fund "BCSI.", mss. V, vol.. 95, 23 May 1939.
BCSI (1941). "Raportul general / General Report". In *J.B.C.S.I.*, May – Aug. 1941, Year IX, , pp. 272 – 274.
BCSI (1942). *Naidăș II*. M.B.M.A. Fund "C. Grofșorean", inv. 8117/59.
BCSI (1944). *Adresă I.S.B.C. – Ministerul de Justiție / Notification of BCSI to the Ministry of Justice*. In T.C.L., Fund "BCSI.", mss. V, vol. 94, no. 139/1944, f.11.
Birăescu, T. (1942). "Patru comune almăjene. Cercetări monografice la Borlovenii Noi, Bozovici, Moceriș și Bănia / Four Almăj commune. Monographic researches at Borlovenii Noi, Bozovici, Moceriș and Bănia". In J.B.C.S.I., year X (Sept. – Dec. 1942), pp. 563 – 594.
Birăescu, T. (1942). *Sănătatea comunei Naidăș / Health of the Naidăș commune*. M.B.M.A., Fund "C. Grofșorean", no. 8087.
Birăescu, T. (1942). *Comuna Naidăș în lumina cifrelor / The commune of Naidăș in the light of figures*. M.B.M.A, Fund "C. Grofșorean", no. 8331.
Boran, Gh. (1939). "Raport monografic asupra școlii primare de stat din Ohaba Bistra / Monographic report on the state primary school of Ohaba Bistra". In J. B.C.S.I., year VII (Jan. – March 1939), no. 25, pp. 21 – 42.
Botiș, E. (1940). "Urbanizarea țăranului român / Urbanisation of the Romanian peasant". In J.B.C.S.I., year VIII (Nov. – Dec. 1940), no. 37 – 38, pp. 639 – 652.
Botiș, E. (1942a). "În pragul unui deceniu de activitate a ISBC / On the threshold of one decade of BCSI activity". In J.B.C.S.I., year X (Jan. – Feb. 1942), pp. 1 – 2.
Botiș, E. (1942a). "În pragul unui deceniu de activitate a ISBC / On the threshold of one decade of BCSI activity". In J.B.C.S.I., year X (Jan. – Feb. 1942), p. 4.
Botiș, E. (1942b). "Raportul Redacției / Report of the editorial board". In J. B.C.S.I., year X (May – Aug. 1942), p. 315.

Bucătură, M. (1940). "Şcoala şi educaţia poporului din Almăj / School and people's education in Almăj". In J.B.C.S.I., year VIII, (May – Jun. 1940), no. 31 – 32, pp. 344 – 351.

Burlacu, C. (1941). "Cronica istorică a Almăjului / Historic chronicle of the Almăj" In J.B.C.S.I., year IX (Jan. – Apr. 1941), pp. 33 – 46.

Burlacu, C. (1942a). "Cronica istorică a Almăjului / Historic chronicle of the Almăj" In J.B.C.S.I., year X (Jan. – Feb. 1942), pp. 58 – 78.

Burlacu, C. (1942b). "Cronica istorică a Almăjului / Historic chronicle of the Almăj" In J.B.C.S.I., year X (March – Apr. 1942), pp. 225 – 235.

Caraion, P. (1971). "Profesorul Dimitrie Gusti şi Şcoala sociologică de la Bucureşti / Professor Dimitrie Gusti and the Bucharest Sociologic School". In *Sociologia Militans,* vol. IV, MCMLXXI, serie îngrijită de / ed. by Pompiliu Caraion. Bucureşti: Editura Ştiinţifică / Bucharest: Scientific Editions.

Chipea, F. (2008). "The contribution of the Romanian sociologist, Dimitrie Gusti to the assertion of sociology as a science of social reality". In the Journal *Annals of the Oradea University*, Gascicle Sociology-Philosophy-Social work, no. VII, Oradea: Editura Universităţii din Oradea / Oradea University Press.

Cocârlan, P. (1941). "Introducere în studiul economico-social al satului Ohaba Bistra / Introduction to the economic-social study of the Ohaba Bistra village". In *J.B.C.S.I.*, year IX (May – Aug. 1941), pp. 215 – 277.

Constantinescu, M., Bădina, O., Gall, E. (1974). *Gîndirea sociologică din România / Romanian sociologic thinking.* Bucureşti: Editura Didactică şi Pedagogică / Bucharest: Didactic and Pedagogic Editions.

Contrea A. (1939). *Cadrul fizic şi etic al unui sat bănăţean / Physical and ethical frame of a Banat village.* Timişoara: Tipografia / Printing House "Sontagsblatt".

Cosma, A. (1942). *Scrisoare Dr. Aurel Cosma jr. către Dr. C. Grofşorean.* M.B.M., Fond "C. Grofşorean", (22 May 1942), MD 34/9745.

Costa-Foru, X. (1945). *Cercetarea monografică a familiei. Contribuţie metodologică / Monographic research of the family. Methodological contribution.* Bucureşti: Fundaţia Regele Mihai / Bucharest: King Mihai Foundation.

Cotoşman, Gh. (1942). "Din trecutul comunei Ohaba Bistra / Of the past of the Ohaba Bistra commune". In *J.B.C.S.I.*, year X (Sept. – Dec. 1942), pp. 620 – 629.

Diaconu, M. (2000). *Şcoala sociologică a lui Dimitrie Gusti. Documentar sociologic / Sociologic school of Dimitrie Gusti. Sociologic documentary*, vol. I: 1880 – 1933, Bucureşti / Bucharest: Editura / Editions Eminescu.

Golopenţia, A., Georgescu, D. C. (1999). *60 sate româneşti / Sixty Romanian villages*. Bucureşti / Bucharest: Editura / Editions Paideia.

Grofşorean, C. (1932). *Expunere de motive privitoare la înfiinţarea ISBC / Motives for the establishment of the BCSI.* , In T.C.L., Mss V, 180, Jan. 1932, f. 2 – 4.

Grofşorean, C. (1937). "Campania monografică din Pojejena de Jos / Monographic campaign in Pojejena de Jos". In *J.B.C.S.I.*., year V, no. 19 – 20, p. 115.

Grofşorean, C. (1938). *Scrisoare C. Grofşorean către D. Gusti / Letter of C. Grofşorean to D. Gusti* . T.C.L., Fund "B.C.S.I.", mss. V, vol. 10, 28 July 1938, f. 32.

Grofşorean, C. (1938). "Raport C. Grofşorean / C. Grofşorean Report". In *J.B.C.S.I.*, Official part, no. 24, p. 125.

Grofşorean, C. (1938). "Metoda monografică a ISBC / BCSI monographic method". In *Timpul*, IX, p. 10.

Grofşorean, C. (1939). *Scrisoare C. Grofşorean – D. Gusti / Letter of C. Grofşorean to D. Gusti.* State's Archives Caransebeş, Reşiţa County Museum Fund, (18 Apr. 1939), no. 132/487/5.

Grofşorean, C. (1940). "În ţara dacilor / In the Dacians' country". In *J.B.C.S.I.*, year VIII (Jan. 1940), no. 27, pp. 1 – 12.

Grofşorean, C. (1941). "În Valea Dunării / In the Danube Valley". In *J.B.C.S.I.*, year IX (Sept. – Dec. 1941), pp. 356 – 374.

Grofşorean, C. (1942). *Raport etico-juridic / Ethical-legal report.* M.B.M.A., Fund "C. Grofşorean", no. 8110/52.

Grofşorean, C. (1942). "Influenţa industrializării asupra ţăranului român / Influence of industrialisation on the Romanian peasant". In *J.B.C.S.I.*, year X (Jan. – Feb. 1942), pp. 144 – 146.

Grofşorean, C. (1942a). "La porţile de fier ale Ardealului / At Ardeal Iron Gates". In *J.B.C.S.I.*, year X (March – Apr. 1942), p. 156.

Grofşorean, C. (1942b). "La porţile de fier ale Ardealului / At Ardeal Iron Gates". In *J.B.C.S.I.*, year X (Sept. – Dec. 1942), p. 639.

Grofşorean, C. (1943). "Un cuib de vulturi daco-valah / A Dacian-Wallachian eagles' nest". In *J.B.C.S.I.*, year XI (May – June 1943), pp. 221 – 279.

Grofşorean, C. (1944). *Scrisoare C. Grofşorean către D. Gusti / Letter of C. Grofşorean to D. Gusti.* D.J.C.S.A.N, Fund "Reşiţa County Museum", (18 March 1944), inv. 582.

Gusti, D. (1924). "Program pentru organizarea vieţii universitare / Programme for the organisation of university life". *"Archive for the social science and reform"*, year V, no. 1 – 2, pp. 174 – 191.

Gusti, D. (1932). "Sociologia. Schiţa unui sistem de sociologie / Sociology. Diagram of a system of sociology". *Revista română de filozofie / Romanian Journal of Philosophy*, vol. XVII, Bucharest, in the vol. *Omagiul profesorului C. Rădulescu-Motru / Homage of Professor C. Rădulescu-Motru*, p. 318.

Gusti, D. (1933). *Înfiinţarea Institutului Social / Establishment of the Banat –Crişana Social Institute.* In *J.B.C.S.I.*, year I (1933), no. 1, p. 33.

Gusti, D. (1936). "Temeiurile teoretice ale cercetărilor monografice / Theoretic grounds of monographic researches". In *"Sociologie Românească / Romanian Sociology"*, Year I (July – Sep. 1936), No. 7 – 9.

Gusti, D. (1936). "Cercetări parţiale şi cercetări integrale sociale / Social partial and integral researches". In *Sociologie Românească / Romanian Sociology*, Year I (Oct. 1936), No. 10.

Gusti, D. (1938). "Legea pentru înfiinţarea Serviciului social / Law for the establishment of the Social Service". In *"Căminul Cultural / The Cultural Home"*, year IV, no. 9, art.4, p. 398.

Gusti, D. (1938). "Principiile sociale şi etnice ale Serviciului social" – lecţie la Facultatea de litere şi filozofie din noiembrie / Social and ethnical principles of the Social Service – lesson given at the Faculty of letters and philosophy in November. In *"Căminul Cultural / Cultural Home"*, year IV, no. 11 – 12, pp. 573 – 574.

Gusti, D. (1939). *Sociologie românească / Romanian sociology,* Year IV (Apr. – June 1939), No. 4 – 6.

Gusti, D. (1940). *Problema sociologiei. Sistem și metodă / Problem of sociology. System and method*. In *Memoriile secțiunii istorice / Memoirs of the historic section*, 3rd series, vol. XXII, Academia Română, București / The Romanian Academy, Bucharest.

Gusti, D. (1943). *Scrisoare D. Gusti – C. Grofșorean / Letter of D. Gusti to C. Grofșorean,* M.B.M. Fund "C. Grofșorean", (1 July 1943), MD 35/9756.

Gusti, D. (1965). *Pagini alese / Selected pages.* București: Editura Științifică / Bucharest: Scientific Editions.

Gusti, D. (1968). *Opere I / Works I.* București: Editura Academiei Republicii Socialiste România / Bucharest: Editions of the Romanian Academy.

Gusti, D. (1969). *Opere II / Works II.* București: Editura Academiei Republicii Socialiste România / Bucharest: Editions of the Romanian Academy.

Gusti, D. (1970). *Opere IV / Works IV.* București: Editura Academiei Republicii Socialiste România / Bucharest: Editions of the Romanian Academy.

Gusti, D. (1971). *Opere V / Works V.* București: Editura Academiei Republicii Socialiste România / Bucharest: Editions of the Romanian Academy.

Gusti, D. (1999). *Școala monografică, Dimitrie Gusti – Știința realității sociale / Monographic school, Dimitrie Gusti – Science of social reality*, vol. I, Collection of the Restitution Fund, paper published with the support of the National Agency for Science, Technology and Innovation, Editions Paideia, Bucharest.

Gusti, D., Herseni, T. (1942). *Elemente de sociologie / Elements of sociology.* București / Bucharest: Editura / Editions Cartea Românească.

Gusti, D., Herseni, T., Stahl, H.H. (1999). *Monografia – teorie și metodă / The monograph – theory and method.* București / Bucharest: Editura / Editions Paideia. paper published with the support of the National Agency for Science, Technology and Innovation.

Herseni, T. (1929). "*Metoda monografică în sociologie / The monographic method in sociology*". In *Societatea de mâine / Tomorrow's society,* year VI (1 – 15 Sept. 1929), no. 16 – 17.

Herseni, T. (1932). *Arhiva pentru știința și reforma socială / Archive for social science and reform,* year X, no. 1 – 4, p. 573.
Herseni, T. (1939). *Adresă Tr. Herseni-Regionala Banat / Notification of Tr. Herseni to the Banat Regional Branch.* T.C.L., Fund "BCSI", mss. V, vol. 95, no. 28208/1939.
Herseni, T. (1939). *Adresă Tr. Herseni-Regionala Banat / Notification of Tr. Herseni to the Banat Regional Branch.* T.C.L., Fund "BCSI", File 27, Notifications of June 21st and 24th 1939.
Herseni, T. (1940). "Plan pentru convorbirile sociologice / Plan for sociologic conversations". In D. Gusti (ed.), *Îndrumări pentru monografiile sociologice / Guidelines for sociologic monographs.* București: Institutul de Științe Sociale al României / Bucharest: Romania's Institute of Social Sciences.
Herseni, T. (1982). *Sociologie. Teoria generală a vieții sociale / Sociology. General theory of social life.* București: Editura Științifică și Enciclopedică / Bucharest: Scientific and Encyclopaedic Editions.
Herseni, T. (2007). *Curs de sociologie rurală / Course of lectures in rural sociology.* București / Bucharest: Editura / Editions Renaissance.
Ilca I. (1942). "Raport coregrafic la Ohaba Bistra / Choreographic report at Ohaba Bistra" . In *J.B.C.S.I.*, year X (Jan. – Feb. 1942), pp. 122 – 126.
Jivan, I. (1940). "Situația din Clisură și Litigiul româno-sârb / The situation on the Danube Shore region and the Romanian-Serbian litigation" (prima parte / first part). In *J.B.C.S.I.*, year VIII (Nov. – Dec. 1940), no. 37 – 38, pp. 653 – 662.
Jivan, I. (1941). "Situația din Clisură și Litigiul româno-sârb sârb / The situation on the Danube Shore region and the Romanian-Serbian litigation" (a doua parte / second part). In *J.B.C.S.I.*, year IX (Jan. – Apr. 1941), pp. 119 – 132.
Larionescu, M. (coord.). (1996). *Școala sociologică de la București. Tradiție și actualitate / Bucharest Sociologic School. Tradition and present relevance.* București / Bucharest: Editura / Editions Metropol.
Larionescu, M. (2007). *Istoria sociologiei românești / History of Romanian sociology.* București / Bucharest: Editura Universității din București / Bucharest University Press.
Larionescu, M. (2007). "Modelele dezvoltării sociale în istoria sociologiei românești / Models of social development on the history of

Romania sociology". In Zamfir, C., Stănescu, S. (coord). (2007). *Enciclopedia dezvoltării sociale / Encyclopaedia of social development*. Iași: Editura / Editions Polirom.

Marian-Jaleș, M. (1942). "Igiena socială a copilului în Ohaba Bistra / Social hygiene of the child at Ohaba Bistra". In *J.B.C.S.I.*, year X (Jan. – Feb. 1942), pp. 127 – 129.

Marinescu, C. (1995). *Dimitrie Gusti și școala sa. Însemnări-Evocări / Dimitrie Gusti and his school. Notes. Evocations*. București: / Bucharest, Editura / Editions "Felix Film", Seria / Series "Restitutio".

Mănoiu, F., Epureanu, V. (1996). *Asistența socială în România / Social work and assistance in Romania*. București / Bucharest: Editura / Editions ALL.

Mosely, P.E. (1936). "The Sociological School of Dimitrie Gusti". În *The Sociological Review*, p. 165.

Neamțu, O. (1970). *Cunoaștere sociologică și acțiune social-culturală în mediul rural / Sociologic knowledge and social-cultural action in the rural environment*. f.e., Oradea.

Neamțu, O. (1971). "Serviciul Social / The Social Service". In *Sociologia Militans, Școala Sociologică de la București / Bucharest Sociologic School,* vol. III, MCMLXXI, București: Editura Științifică / Bucharest: Scientific Editions, serie îngrijită de / ed. by Pompiliu Caraion.

Nedelea, V. (1938), "Raport general asupra activității monografice din comuna Ohaba Bistra / General report on the monographic activity in the Ohaba Bistra commune". In *J.B.C.S.I.*, year VI (Oct. – Dec.1838), no. 24, pp. 130 – 138.

Negru, A. (1999). *Din istoria cercetării sociale românești. Institutul Social Banat Crișana / From the history of the Romania social research. The Banat Crișana Social Institute*. Cluj-Napoca: Editura / Editions Argonaut.

Negru, I. (1943). "Statistica Clisurii de Sus / Statistics of the Upper Danube Shore". In *J.B.C.S.I.*, year XI (Jan. – Apr. 1943), p. 29.

Nemoianu, I. (1942). "Pe marginea jubileului ISBC / About the BCSI jubilee". In *J.B.C.S.I.*, year X (May – Aug. 1942), p. 283.

Nemoianu, I. (1942). "Pe marginea jubileului ISBC / About the BCSI jubilee". In *J.B.C.S.I.*, year X (May – Aug. 1942), p. 295.

Otovescu, D. (coord.) (2006). *Monografia sociologică în România. Cercetări contemporane / Sociologic monograph in Romania. Contemporary researches.* Craiova: Editura / Editions Beladi.

Rostás, Z. (2005). *Atelierul gustian / The Gustian Workshop.* București: / Bucharest Editura /Editions Tritonic.

RSI (1927). *Arhiva pentru știința și reforma socială / Archive for social science and reform.* year. VI, no. 3 – 4, p. 525.

Secoșan, E. (1938). "O nouă subsecțiune a Institutului / A new subsection of the Institute". In *J.B.C.S.I.,* year VI (1938), no. 24, p. 134.

Secoșan, E. (1940a). "Izvoare almăjene / Almăj sources". In *J.B.C.S.I.,* year VIII (Feb. – March 1940), no. 28 – 29, pp. 115 – 133.

Secoșan, E. (1940b). "Izvoare almăjene / Almăj sources". In *J.B.C.S.I.,* year VIII (May – June 1940), no. 31 – 32, pp. 339 – 343.

Stahl, H.H. (coord.). (1980). *Dimitrie Gusti, Studii critice / Dimitrie Gusti, Critical studies.* București: Editura Științifică și Enciclopedică / Bucharest: Scientific and Encyclopaedic Editions.

Stahl, H.H. (1971). "Învățămintele metodice și tehnice / Methodological and technical lessons". In *Sociologia Militans, Școala Sociologică de la București / Bucharest Sociologic School,* vol. III, MCMLXXI, București: Editura Științifică / Bucharest: Scientific Editions, serie îngrijită de / ed. by Pompiliu Caraion.

Stahl, H.H. (2001). *Tehnica monografiei sociologice / Technique of sociologic monograph.* București / Bucharest: Editura / Editions S.N.S.P.A., Facultatea de Comunicare și Relații Publice "David Ogilvy" / Faculty of Communication and Public Relations "David Ogilvy" , ediție îngrijită de / ed. by Septimiu Chelcea.

Stahl, P.H. (2000). *Triburi și sate din sud-estul Europei / Tribes and villages of south-eastern Europe.* București / Bucharest: Editura / Editions Paideia.

Stănoiu, A., Voinea, M. (1983). *Sociologia familiei / Sociology of the family.* București / Bucharest: Tipografia Universității București / Bucharest University Printing House.

Stângu, Tr. (1942). "Raport juridic din comuna Ohaba Bistra / Legal report of the Ohaba Bistra commune". In *J.B.C.S.I.,* year X (March – Apr. 1942), pp. 236 – 249.

Stiniguță, I. (1940a). "Valea Almăjului / The Almăj Valley". In *J.B.C.S.I.,* year VIII (Jan. 1940), no. 27, p. 25 – 32.

Stiniguță, I. (1940b). "Valea Almăjului / The Almăj Valley". In *J.B.C.S.I.*, year VIII (Feb. – March 1940), no. 28 – 29, pp. 134 – 142.

Șora, M. (1941). "Viața religioasă și morală din comuna Pojejena română / Religious and moral life in the Romanian Pojejena commune". In *J.B.C.S.I.*, year IX (Jan. – Apr. 1941), pp. 47 – 57.

Șora, M. (1943). "Viața religioasă și morală din comuna Pojejena română / Religious and moral life in the Romanian Pojejena commune". In *J.B.C.S.I.*, year (June 1943), pp. 419 – 442.

Ursu, N. (1938). "Folclor muzical din comuna Ohaba Bistra / Musical folklore of the Ohaba Bistra commune". In *J.B.C.S.I.*, year VI (Oct. – Dec. 1938), no. 24, pp. 111 – 115.

Ursu, N. (1940). "O nuntă în valea Almăjului / A wedding in the Almăj Valley". In *J.B.C.S.I.*, year VIII (July – Oct. 1940), no. 33 – 36, pp. 469 – 494.

Vedinaș, T. (2001). *Introducere în sociologia rurală / Introduction to rural sociology*. Iași: Editura / Editions Polirom.

Vulcănescu, M. (1929). "Satul românesc / The Romanian village". In *Realitatea ilustrată / Illustrated reality*, year II (28 Sept. 1929), no. 40, pp. 3 – 11.

Vulcănescu, M. (1998). *Școala sociologică a lui Dimitrie Gusti / Dimitrie Gusti's Sociologic School*. București / Bucharest: Editura / Editions Eminescu. Ediție îngrijită de / ed. by Marin Diaconu.

Zamfir, C. (2005). "Ce a lăsat Dimitrie Gusti sociologiei postbelice? / What did Dimitrie Gusti leave to post-war sociology?". In the Journal *Sociologie Românească / Romanian Sociology,* vol III, no. 2, p. 11.

Zamfir, E. (1999). "Sistemul serviciilor de asistență socială în România / "System of social work services in Romania. In the vol. Zamfir, C., (coord.), *Politici sociale în România: 1990 – 1998 / Social policies in Romania: 1990 – 1998*. București / Bucharest: Editura / Editions Expert.

Zamfir, E. (2004). "Relansarea profesiei de asistent social în România, condiție esențială în promovarea incluziunii sociale / Relaunching of the social worker profession in Romania, essential condition for the promotion of social inclusion". In the vol. Chipea, F., Ștefănescu, F., (coord.), *Combaterea sărăciei și promovarea incluziunii sociale / Fight against poverty and promotion of social inclusion,* Oradea: Editura Universității din Oradea. / Oradea University Press

Annex

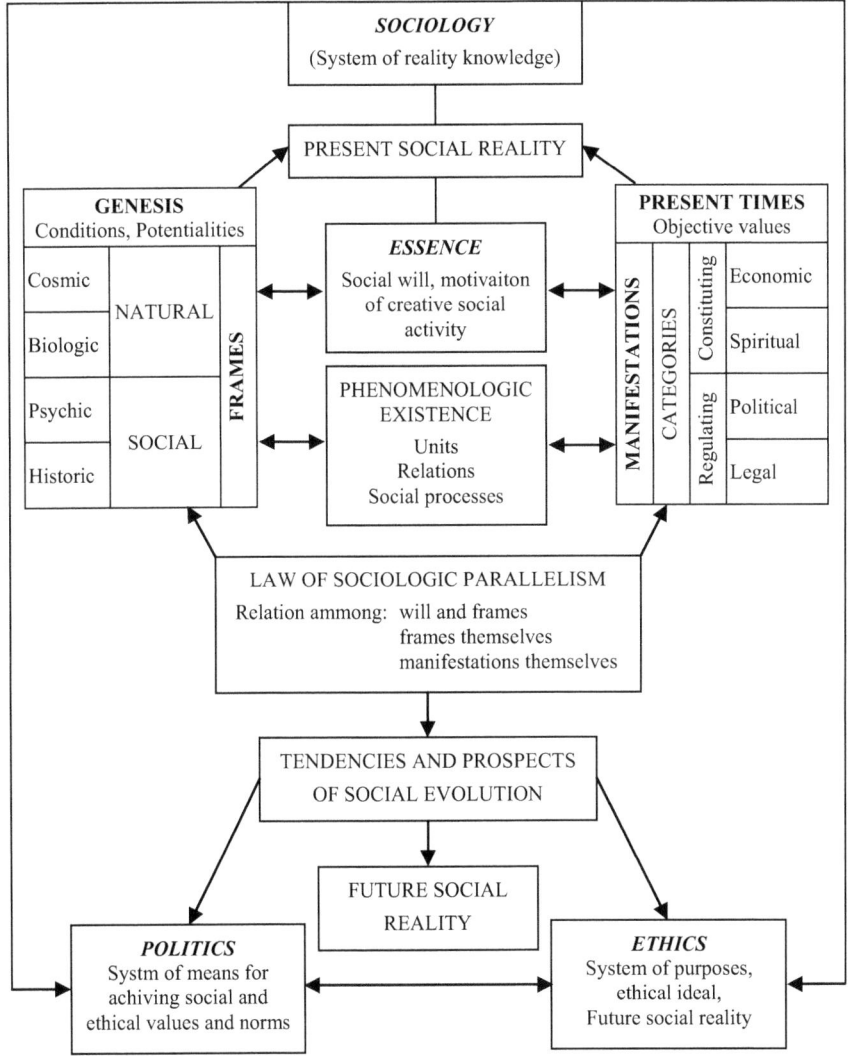

Fig. 1.1. Dimitrie Gusti. System of sociology, ethics and politics
Source: Gusti, D., 1968, p. 237